CONSTITUTIONAL PERSONAE

Not a Suicide Pact
The Constitution in a Time of National Emergency
Richard A. Posner

Supreme Neglect
How to Revive Constitutional Protection for Private Property
Richard A. Epstein

Out of Range
Why the Constitution Can't End the Battle over Guns
Mark V. Tushnet

Unfinished Business
Racial Equality in American History
Michael J. Klarman

Is There a Right to Remain Silent?
Coercive Interrogation and the Fifth Amendment After 9/11
Alan M. Dershowitz

The Invisible Constitution
Laurence H. Tribe

Uninhibited, Robust, and Wide-Open
A Free Press for a New Century
Lee C. Bollinger

From Disgust to Humanity
Sexual Orientation and Constitutional Law
Martha C. Nussbaum

The Living Constitution
David A. Strauss

Keeping Faith with the Constitution
Goodwin Liu, Pamela S. Karlan, and Christopher H. Schroeder

Cosmic Constitutional Theory
Why Americans Are Losing Their Inalienable Right to Self-Governance
J. Harvie Wilkinson III

More Essential Than Ever
The Fourth Amendment in the Twenty-First Century
Stephen J. Schulhofer

On Constitutional Disobedience
Louis Michael Seidman

The Twilight of Human Rights Law
Eric A. Posner

Constitutional Personae

. . .

Cass R. Sunstein

OXFORD
UNIVERSITY PRESS

OXFORD

UNIVERSITY PRESS

Oxford University Press is a department of the University of
Oxford. It furthers the University's objective of excellence
in research, scholarship, and education by publishing worldwide.

Published in the United States of America by
Oxford University Press
198 Madison Avenue, New York, NY 10016

© Cass R. Sunstein 2015

Library of Congress Cataloging-in-Publication Data
Sunstein, Cass R. author.
Constitutional personae / Cass R. Sunstein.
pages cm
"The leading Personae are Heroes, Soldiers, Minimalists, and Mutes" — Chapter one.
ISBN 978-0-19-022267-3 (hardback : alk. paper)
1. Constitutional law—United States. I. Title.
KF4550.S833 2015
342.73—dc23

2015002226

1 3 5 7 9 8 6 4 2
Printed in the United States of America on acid-free paper

Contents

. . .

CONTENTS

Editor's Note

. . .

We hold these truths to be self-evident, that all men are created
equal, that they are endowed by their Creator with certain unalien-
able Rights....

—The Declaration of Independence

THE SUPREME COURT is, of course, central to our understanding of
our inalienable rights. It therefore follows that, to understand those
rights, we must understand the Supreme Court. In *Constitutional
Personae*, Cass Sunstein illuminates the behavior of both the justices
and the Supreme Court as an institution. He first explores the different stances that justices take to the challenge of constitutional decision making. Although these stances (or "Personae") may vary even for
the same justice from one case to the next, Sunstein astutely observes
that, in any given case involving constitutional interpretation, justices tend to adopt the character of Heroes, Soldiers, Minimalists, or
Mutes. These Personae do not necessarily correspond to any particular
theory of constitutional interpretation or to any particular "liberal" or

"conservative" ideology. Rather, they are independently revealing of the self-presentation of the justices on a case-by-case basis, and they shed interesting light on the various ways in which the justices cast their own roles as they undertake the task of giving content to our constitutional rights.

Sunstein next turns his attention to the distinct, but related, question of constitutional interpretation. He examines the primary methodologies of constitutional interpretation and argues that, in evaluating any particular methodology, it is important to take into account the decision and error costs. That is, what are the risks, under any particular approach to interpretation, that the justices will get it wrong, and what are the costs of such errors? Sunstein concludes that these risks, and the merits of competing interpretative approaches, may vary significantly from one case to another, depending on the nature of the issue to be resolved. He therefore suggests that there is no one "right" method of constitutional interpretation and no one "right" Constitutional Personae. Because the Constitution does not itself dictate any particular mode of interpretation or Constitutional Personae, "the meaning of the Constitution must be made rather than found," and "any approach to the document must be defended by some account that is defended by the interpreter."

Sunstein next turns to that very task himself, defending his own preferred mode of constitutional interpretation—minimalism. Although acknowledging that there are reasoned objections to the Minimalist Personae, he concludes, relying on the work of Edmund Burke, that "constitutional principles must be built incrementally and by analogy, and with close reference to longstanding practices." He identifies Felix Frankfurter and Sandra Day O'Connor as the two justices who best exemplify this approach, and he explains in a careful analysis why, in his view, this stance, in the long run, best serves the interests of the nation.

Finally, Sunstein considers the behavior of the Court itself as an institution. He shows that the Court changed fundamentally in 1941.

Before then, the Court was rarely divided, there were relatively few dissenting opinions, and the various Personae of the justices were largely undeveloped. Since then, however, division within the Court has become much more common, leading not only to the evolution of the four distinct Personae but also to profound changes in the functioning of the Court and in the understanding of its role in American democracy. Sunstein explains why this shift occurred and explores its implications both for the Court and the nation in the future.

In sum, in *Constitutional Personae* Cass Sunstein offers new insights, raises new questions, poses novel explanations, and enriches our understanding of our inalienable rights.

Geoffrey R. Stone
October 2015

Preface

. . .

OUR IMAGINATIONS, MORAL and otherwise, are populated by identifiable types of people. Whether the subject is politics or sports, medicine or law, war-making or peace-making, romance or friendship, human beings tend to be attracted to particular types.

Some of us are drawn to personalities that others abhor. Maybe you like those who break the rules and buck traditions, or maybe you fear and even despise them. Some people admire swashbucklers, with out-sized personalities and a taste for the dramatic; others prefer elegance, calm, and understatement. Maybe you like people who talk softly (but carry a big stick); maybe you admire those who follow, unerringly and with loyalty and precision, those who are in charge.

Our imaginations are also populated by both heroes and villains, and in literature and life, it may not always be easy to tell the difference between them. The great poet of the unconscious, William Blake, said that in *Paradise Lost*, John Milton "wrote in fetters when he wrote of Angels & God, and at liberty when of Devils & Hell because he was a true Poet and of the Devil's party without knowing it." Blake meant to draw attention to the fact that in Milton's poem, Satan ends up stealing the show. His subversiveness speaks of freedom and flight and a kind of Dionysian joy—a refusal to be cabined and caged. Whether or not true Poets are of the Devil's party, and whether or not they know it, Blake got Milton exactly right.

Does this have anything to do with constitutional law? I think so. A lot of ink has been spilled on appropriate approaches to constitutional interpretation, and we know a great deal about why people might adopt one or another approach. (I will spill more such ink here.) But it is worth considering whether many people are initially drawn to a particular approach not because of the reasons offered on its behalf, but because of the sensibility, or the Persona, that the approach asks judges to assume. In politics and law, some of us are attracted to heroes, because of their sheer size and capacity for greatness; others find heroes a bit alarming, because they can be arrogant, grandiose, disrespectful, full of themselves, and ultimately destructive. In politics and law, some of us find humility a signal virtue, whereas others find it a kind word for timidity and cowardice.

The economist Lawrence Summers speaks of people's "characterological direction of error," meaning the direction of the mistakes that they will make, given their particular characters. Summers's phrase is a bit awkward, but it is profoundly illuminating. In the United States, Richard Nixon's characterological direction of error was corruption—the dark side of his immense shrewdness and his keen strategic sense. Ronald Reagan's was obliviousness and negligence—the dark side of his appealing sunniness. In law and politics, heroic figures may suffer from hubris and create tragedies. (Shakespeare's plays probe people's characterological direction of error.) For their part, humble figures may be cowards; they might capitulate to evil. When people are drawn to a sensibility or a Persona, it is often because its characterological direction of error does not much trouble them; it might even delight them. Milton is a case in point.

My principal claims, then, are that constitutional law is populated by identifiable Personae and that often a Persona has an immediate or intuitive appeal, so that the justifications offered on its behalf turn out to be after-the-fact rationalizations—the tail wagging the dog. The suggestion is a speculation, a hypothesis, and it remains to be tested. In fact, we could easily imagine empirical research that would do so. My initial goal here is not to offer such research, but instead to identify the four Constitutional Personae, to set out their inclinations, to show their appeal, and to put them in dialogue with one another. I am hopeful that the exercise will help to illuminate constitutional debates as they have unfolded over time—and as they will continue for the indefinite future, not only in the United States but throughout the world.

I have a second goal as well, and it is equally important. Many people believe that their preferred approach to constitutional interpretation—and hence the Persona or Personae that they adopt—follows from an account of what interpretation is. On this view, the very idea of interpretation carries with it a certain compulsion, which directs us toward a particular approach and a particular Persona. There is a kernel of truth in this view. If you are interpreting a text, you cannot simply abandon it or understand it to mean whatever you like. There are some things that interpretation just isn't. But interpreters are free to adopt many different approaches, while also remaining interpreters. The choice of approach is inescapably ours.

How shall we make that choice? It is helpful, even indispensable, to acknowledge that no approach makes sense in every imaginable world. Any answer depends on a claim *about what will make the constitutional order better*, and hence about the capacities of different institutions—about which is likely to perform well and which is likely to perform badly. I suggest that if we begin with a simple framework, focused on the costs of decisions and the costs of errors, we will be able to make a lot of progress. By the costs of decisions, I mean the burdens of actually resolving problems. By the costs of errors, I mean to refer to the number and the magnitude of mistakes. I hope to show that when people adopt a particular approach to interpretation, or favor a particular Persona, it is because of an assumption, or an argument, that their approach will reduce the sum of decision costs and error costs (with an emphasis on the latter)—and that an understanding of this simple point will help explain what people are actually disagreeing about.

True, the idea of costs of decision needs a lot of discussion, and the idea of costs of errors is even more challenging. But my hope is that the two ideas will, in the end, help explain what people who disagree about constitutional law, and about the right Persona, are really disagreeing about.

But let's put our cards on the table. My third goal is to elaborate the approach, and the Persona, that I tend to like best. For judges engaged in constitutional law, my preferred Persona is the Minimalist, whose defining commitments grow out of the work of the British social theorist Edmund Burke. Minimalism is not a full theory of interpretation, and it is not an approach for all times and seasons. But it has particular appeal in the context of American constitutional law, or so I shall suggest.

As we shall also see, there are two varieties of minimalism. One of them demands reasons and requires the government to justify its practices. The other (and the more Burkean) emphasizes traditions and sees traditions as justifications. Both of these approaches have their place. In cases that involve rights—such as the right to equal protection of the laws—a form of rationalist minimalism is best. In deciding whether and when discrimination is acceptable, judges should not merely follow traditions. In cases that involve separation of powers—asking, for example, about the authority of the president—Burkean minimalism is the right place to begin (and often to end). The reason is that for institutional matters, long-settled practices deserve a great deal of respect; judges should be reluctant to disturb them.

The remainder of the book is presented in four chapters. The first, and the most important, outlines the four Personae and their relationship to theories of constitutional law. The second explores the nature of interpretation and claims that inevitably, we must make our own choices about the best approach. That is a modest claim, in the sense that it leaves room for all four Personae, and also for a wide variety of approaches to constitutional law, ranging from Justice Antonin Scalia's form of originalism to Justice Stephen Breyer's emphasis on "active liberty." Nonetheless, it is essential to see that the central choices are our own, and that certain claims about interpretation—some of them intuitively convincing—mask the necessity of choice, and thus of some effort, by any interpreter, to justify the approach that he is adopting.

The third chapter turns to Burkean minimalism and offers a qualified endorsement. It emphasizes that in all its forms, minimalism shows an appropriate degree of modesty—and that small steps are often the right steps. At the same time, it argues that some minimalists require reasons, not merely longstanding practices, and that they are often right to do so. A principal goal of the chapter is to demonstrate that no Persona, and no approach, makes sense in the abstract, or under all imaginable circumstances. A great deal depends on the capacities of various institutions—on judgments about which is likely to err, and how badly.

To understand the Personae, it is important to have a historical perspective and to understand when the justices feel free to speak in their own voice, rather than merely joining the majority. The final chapter investigates those questions. Among other things, it shows that those who embrace judicial unanimity, and seek to reduce internal dissent, tend to have minimalist inclinations. In the end, however, it concludes that the standard arguments in favor of unanimity, and against internal dissent, are unconvincing. Publicly expressed disagreement within the Court can be desirable, because of the information that it provides to future courts, to legislators, and to the public as a whole. The continuing arguments among the various Personae—visible for all to see—are a great service to the nation.

The book closes with a brief note on rules of attraction—on why people are drawn to one or another Persona. One of my principal claims throughout is that the choice depends on the right theory of constitutional interpretation. If you believe that the meaning of the Constitution evolves over time, you will often embrace soldiering for that very reason. If you believe that the role of the Supreme Court is to protect endangered minorities, you will be drawn to heroism. At the same time, it is true that people often have a strong psychological attachment to one of the Personae—and immediate skepticism about, or even revulsion toward, the others. These psychological attachments can precede, and outrun, theories of interpretation. As we shall see, the same is true in the domain of politics as well. As in life, and as in law, so in democracy: People are drawn to identifiable types. That can be a serious problem, but it is an enduring fact in self-governing societies.

CHAPTER ONE

Constitutional Personae

Is THE CONSTITUTION living or dead? Should judges follow the original understanding of the Constitution, even if it offers little protection for individual rights? Should judges defer to political majorities, even if they appear to invade such rights? Should judges follow longstanding traditions, even if they seem oppressive? Should they attempt to improve democratic processes—for example, by giving special protection to the right to vote and the right to free speech? Should they offer moral readings of the founding document—for example, by invoking the best understandings of equality and liberty? Should they pay attention to social movements and try to adopt what is best in them?

The differences among competing theories of constitutional interpretation are of course fundamental. But if we investigate the arc of constitutional history, we will discover another set of differences. They involve disparate *Constitutional Personae*—judicial roles and self-presentations that sharply separate judges as well as those who comment on their work.

The leading Personae are Heroes, Soldiers, Minimalists, and Mutes. Broadly speaking, Heroes are willing and sometimes even eager to invoke the Constitution to strike down federal and state legislation. They are comfortable with big, bold strokes. By contrast, Soldiers are humble. They like to take orders. They defer to the actions of the political branches. They prefer not to strike anything down. If Congress has enacted legislation, Soldiers want to uphold it. Minimalists favor only incremental change. They like small steps. Mutes prefer not to decide difficult questions. They believe that silence is golden.

The four Personae help to define not only internal disputes on the Court but also famous cases and whole eras of Supreme Court history. Countless past and present constitutional disputes involve contests among the Personae. Consider, for example, disputes over same-sex marriage, the Affordable Care Act, campaign finance laws, the Voting Rights Act, recess appointments by the president, and affirmative action. In each of these disputes, and many more, all of the four Personae have played important roles (while also cutting across standard ideological and methodological divisions). We can also identify large periods of Supreme Court heroism, soldiering, and minimalism (though not muteness), certainly with respect to particular constitutional clauses, and sometimes with respect to judicial behavior in general.

Predictions are often hazardous, but it is safe to say that as long as American constitutional law exists, we will see debates among the four Personae. Indeed, we can find the four Personae in many different constitutional systems all over the world. Germany, Canada, South Africa, and Israel—to name just a few—have their own Heroes, Soldiers, Minimalists, and Mutes.

An understanding of the Personae cannot, of course, displace standard theories of constitutional interpretation. As we shall see, the choice of Persona is ultimately dependent on the selection of some such theory, certainly as a matter of logic. Suppose that judges embrace a particular theory—say, originalism, understood to require the provisions of the Constitution to be interpreted in a way that is consistent with their original public meaning at the time that they were ratified. Originalism might lead a judge to be heroic, soldierly, minimalist, or mute, as the controversy and the occasion demand.

I shall devote considerable attention to this point and hence to the relationship between the Personae and competing constitutional theories. Nonetheless, an understanding of the Personae provides a novel and illuminating perspective on recurring constitutional debates (or so I shall attempt to show). We can even see constitutional history as a long series of debates among the Personae.

It is important to emphasize that the Personae are both abstract and stylized and no real-world judge "is" just one or another of them. To be sure, particular judges can be associated with particular Personae, and some judges do show a dominant tendency. But in other cases, any such association might be taken to mean only that on especially prominent occasions, the judge has assumed that Persona, or that the judge shows a tendency to adopt that Persona in the most important and challenging disputes. Over the course of a career or even a year, many real-world judges will adopt more than one of the Personae—and possibly all of them. Some judges switch their Persona from one case to another, because their preferred theory of interpretation calls for such switching. Some justices are Heroes on Tuesday (voting to ban discrimination against same-sex couples) but Soldiers on Thursday (voting to uphold the Affordable Care Act). Other judges have a more or less consistent Persona because their preferred theory calls for it. Still other judges change their stance for strategic or other reasons.

It is important to see that adoption of a Persona need not be opportunistic, cynical, or manipulative. It may well be an authentic reflection of the role that "falls out" of the judge's preferred theory of interpretation. Nonetheless, it cannot be denied that a judge might adopt a Persona as a matter of strategy. For example, a judge might prefer in the abstract to be a Hero, but she might face significant constraints, including judicial precedents, internal dynamics on a multimember court (which require a measure of compromise), or anticipated public reactions. In light of those constraints, she might write as a Minimalist—with the hope that the minimalist path might eventually produce the same result that heroism would dictate. Muteness itself might also be strategic, a form of biding one's time until the time is right. A judge might silence herself in the hope of fighting another day.

In recent years, some people have speculated that Chief Justice John Roberts is playing the "long game," which means that he has a vision of where he wants the Court to go, with heroic components, but that he is prepared to write and to join narrow, minimalist opinions—merely signaling, but not insisting on, the ultimate direction. On this view, he may be a Hero in his heart of hearts, but he is in a kind of minimalist closet. Whether or not the speculation is correct, it is true that some judges will be Minimalist or Mute for strategic reasons, or because the composition of the Court does not allow them to go in the direction that they prefer.

As we shall also see, a Persona might be a reflection of a judge's actual thinking or instead a judge's preferred self-presentation. A judge might write and present herself as a Soldier even though her actual conception of the judicial role is heroic. Few judges are likely to say or think, "I am a Soldier," but a judge might well have an explicit or implicit account of the judicial role that leads to soldierly votes and opinions. Such a judge would be likely to have a soldierly self-presentation, telling the public: "I am just following orders here." Indeed, when judges insist that they are merely following the law, they are assuming the role of the Soldier.

No judge self-identifies as a Mute; that would be ridiculous. But all judges agree that on occasion, silence is a good idea, and when they do, they are self-conscious Mutes. Most judges do have a minimalist conception of their role, at least on certain occasions. And while no judge will announce, "I am a Hero," many judges do believe that the Constitution sets out ambitious principles of one kind or another, and that it is fully appropriate for judges to invoke those principles even if the result is to invalidate legislation. In especially interesting cases, a judge might present himself as a Soldier, merely following the law, and that presentation might even reflect his self-understanding—but the judge might be taken as a Hero in certain communities, even though he is not invalidating anything. If you think the Affordable Care Act is a great idea, you might think that it is heroic for a judge to vote to uphold it. As we will see, a Persona might also reflect not a judge's self-understanding or self-presentation, but how a judge is received by some, many, or all members of the community.

Let's now turn to the four Players.

HEROES

Because of its importance and social salience, the heroic Persona may be the most familiar. The defining characteristic of judicial Heroes is that they are big and bold. They are entirely willing to invoke an ambitious understanding of the Constitution to invalidate the decisions of the federal government and the states. Heroes come in many varieties; there are left-wing heroes and right-wing heroes. Heroes may emphasize equality on the basis of race, sex, and sexual orientation, or they may stress the limited power of the national government and the importance of private property and freedom of contract. But whatever their ideology, and whatever their favored approach to constitutional interpretation, Heroes believe in a large and potentially transformative role for the federal judiciary in the Constitution's name.

Many Heroes look forward to a utopian future—for example, to an imagined era some years from now, when (it is assumed) improved understanding of liberty, privacy, and equality will prevail. Heroes of this kind do not want to be "on the wrong side of history." In the past, Heroes have sought to promote equality on the basis of race, sex, and sexual orientation, thinking that both justice and history are on their side. But restoration of some previous status quo counts as one form of transformation, and some (conservative) Heroes do insist on restoration—for example, to a real or imagined era before the New Deal, or to the period before the 1950s. Some Heroes have considerable sympathy for the words of the conservative William F. Buckley Jr., writing a mission statement in 1955 for the *National Review*, who stated that the magazine "stands athwart history, yelling Stop."

Within the categories of Heroes and heroism, we can find significant differences of degree, from relatively modest Heroes who are willing to strike down acts of Congress without having major reformist aims, to more far-reaching Heroes (Superheroes?) who have large-scale visions and are willing (and perhaps even eager) to embark on significant projects of social change. To sharpen the category, I will generally understand Heroes to have a high degree of theoretical ambition, with an acknowledgment that their ambition may stem from different theories of constitutional interpretation. Wherever they stand, Heroes tend to have large ideas about national power, equality, liberty, property, speech, and sex.

It follows that both originalists and nonoriginalists can be Heroes. We can imagine Second Amendment Heroes, protecting gun rights, and Equal Protection Heroes, protecting against discrimination. Both might draw either on their preferred account of the original understanding or on their favorite moral reading of the relevant provisions. Some Heroes claim to speak for the text and history of the Constitution, but they are actually relying on moral or political theories of their own. Some Heroes are candid about the role of their personal values. Other Heroes are genuinely focused on what they regard as the original understanding.

As I am understanding them here, all Heroes can be considered "activist" in the distinctive sense that they are willing to use the Constitution to strike down acts of Congress and of state legislatures. It is important to see that as used here, the term "heroic," like the term "activist," should not be taken to be one of approval; it is merely a descriptive term. You can certainly reject many or even all forms of judicial heroism. In ordinary language, soldiers can of course be heroes as well, and while I aim to distinguish them here, we shall encounter some interesting alliances and antagonisms between the Hero and the Soldier.

Because of its effects in invalidating racial segregation, *Brown v. Board of Education* is the iconic heroic decision, and its author, Chief Justice Earl Warren, is the iconic heroic judge. Indeed, the period of the Warren Court, generally beloved by the political left and reviled by the right, was the Court's iconic heroic era, helping to define a conception of the federal judiciary for a generation and more. The Court's countless heroic decisions included rulings that called for a rule of one person, one vote; abolished the poll tax; required the *Miranda* warnings; expanded the reach of the constitutional protection against "unreasonable searches and seizures"; and struck down bans on the use of contraceptives. From the 1960s, many people on the left have celebrated the Warren Court and argued for continuation of its distinctive form of heroism. But other eras have been heroic too, and many judges have been heroic, at least on prominent occasions.

John Marshall was the original judicial Hero, at least certainly insofar as *Marbury v. Madison* established the institution of judicial review (enabling the Court to strike down legislation). The *Dred Scott* decision, entrenching the institution of slavery (and forbidding Congress from doing much about it), is an important part of the constitutional "anticanon." Even if it is egregiously wrong, it reflects a large-scale vision of the original constitutional settlement, which it opposes to democratically enacted legislation—and it is unquestionably heroic in the sense in which I am using that term. The *Lochner* era, in which the Court struck down minimum wage and maximum hour legislation, had many heroic moments—even if some of the justices on the *Lochner* Court understood and presented themselves as Soldiers or Minimalists. For decades, Justices William Brennan and Thurgood Marshall counted as exemplary liberal Heroes, involving their preferred understandings of equality and liberty to build on the work of the Warren Court.

With his willingness to offer large pronouncements about such large values as liberty and dignity (often his particular interest), Justice Anthony Kennedy may well be the most heroic member of the current Court. But Antonin Scalia and Clarence Thomas have heroic moments and tendencies, especially in seeking to vindicate Second Amendment rights, to protect commercial advertising, to forbid affirmative action, to strike down restrictions on campaign contributions, and to limit the power of the national government. In recent years, heroic judges, with strong conservative inclinations, have voted to invalidate the Affordable Care Act, campaign finance laws, gun control laws, and affirmative action programs.

Different constitutional provisions provide different occasions for heroism, and Heroes qualify as such with respect to particular provisions, not the Constitution as a whole. Across-the-board heroism, as I am understanding it here, would be difficult to imagine, because it fits with no recognizable theory of constitutional interpretation. There are Free Speech Heroes, Equal Protection Heroes, Due Process Heroes, Religious Liberty Heroes, Fourth Amendment Heroes, Commerce Clause Heroes, Second Amendment Heroes, Executive Power Heroes, Takings Heroes, Standing Heroes, and many more. A judge might endorse heroism with respect to one provision but firmly reject it with respect to others. Indeed, that pattern is common. When the Court as a whole is heroic for certain periods, its heroism can be found only in connection with particular provisions—with, for example, the Warren Court using the First Amendment, the Fourth, Fifth, and Sixth Amendments, and the equal protection clause, and the *Lochner* Court invoking the commerce clause and the due process clause.

Heroism has had enthusiastic academic defenders, above all Ronald Dworkin and John Hart Ely, and both members of the public and academic commentators, whatever their political views, are often inclined to lionize judicial Heroes and to argue for more in the way of heroism. Political activists often favor them. It might even be right to say that for law professors, Heroes are the preferred Persona. But it is important to see that heroism's academic defenders are highly diverse in both their ideological orientation and their theory of interpretation.

I have noted that in the aftermath of the era that *Brown* helped to define, many academic commentators saw that decision as establishing the appropriate judicial role. They hoped for many *Browns*—five, ten, a hundred—vindicating large-scale conceptions of liberty or equality, and reforming society accordingly. In the modern era, those who have long wanted the Court to require states to recognize same-sex marriages can be counted as Hero-worshippers.

Dworkin discusses, with evident admiration, a judge named Hercules, who renders moral judgments while interpreting the broad phrases in the Constitution ("the freedom of speech," "equal protection," "due process of law"). Hercules is the most sustained academic elaboration of the heroic judicial Persona.[1] Emphasizing the heroic role of judges in promoting democratic self-government (for example, by protecting the right to vote), Ely dedicates his influential book to the iconic Hero Earl Warren, specifically observing that "you don't need many heroes if you choose carefully."[2] Those who embrace Ely's theory of judicial review, which calls for an active judiciary in the reinforcement of democracy, are likely to support heroism, at least some of the time. They want the Court to protect groups that are politically weak, or subject to "prejudice," and they also want the Court to police the political process. For these reasons, they will seek and embrace heroic rulings.

More recently, those with a libertarian conception of the Constitution, like law professors Randy Barnett and Richard Epstein, are seeking to promote judicial heroism through aggressive use of certain constitutional provisions in the interest of a particular (and controversial) conception of liberty. They want to promote a broad understanding of the Constitution's takings clause, and thus to expand people's property rights, in a way that would produce a form of heroism. Libertarian constitutional theorists also defend contracts clause heroism, seeking to protect freedom of contract from government interference. Consider too vigorous efforts to limit Congress's power under the commerce clause and the necessary and proper clause, in such a way as to impose serious restrictions on the authority of the national legislature—as exercised, for example, in the enactment of the Affordable Care Act. Notwithstanding those efforts, the Court upheld that act, but further challenges to congressional enactments are inevitable, and litigants will be arguing for heroism. Many modern libertarians argue for a form of heroism that would raise serious doubts about congressional enactments involving civil rights, endangered species, occupational safety, drug regulation, and much more. And of course the Court's decision in *Bush v. Gore*, effectively awarding the presidency to George W. Bush, was heroic in the sense in which I am using the term.

As we shall see below, originalists can certainly be Heroes, and Minimalists can make common cause with Heroes as well (though their minimalism severely qualifies their heroism). For now, the important point is that progressives have often championed judicial heroism of their preferred sort, and that conservatives and libertarians have done exactly the same thing.

SOLDIERS

What Soldiers Do

At the opposite pole from Heroes are Soldiers, who argue in favor of following orders. The defining feature of the judicial Soldier is a willingness to defer to the will of his superiors, typically understood as the political branches of government. In ordinary language, of course, the idea of the Soldier can be understood in many different ways. As I understand them here, Soldiers are humble and deferential, and they understand or portray themselves as *subordinates*, essentially doing what others have told them to do. (Originalists, who also portray themselves as Soldiers, provide an important wrinkle, to which I will turn in due course.)

Justice Oliver Wendell Holmes is a hero to many, and he may well deserve the label. Many people would rank him as the greatest Supreme Court justice that the United States has ever had. But he also fought in the Civil War, and in terms of the Personae, he was largely a Soldier, as reflected in his famous suggestion, "If my fellow citizens want to go to Hell I will help them. It's my job." With his great dissenting words in *Lochner*, arguing for judicial restraint as the Court struck down a maximum hour law, Holmes helped to define the Persona of the Soldier for well over a century: "a constitution is not intended to embody a particular economic theory, whether of paternalism and the organic relation of the citizen to the state or of *laissez faire*. It is made for people of fundamentally differing views, and the accident of our finding certain opinions natural and familiar, or novel, and even shocking, ought not to conclude our judgment upon the question whether statutes embodying them conflict with the Constitution of the United States."[3]

It is important to see that for freedom of speech, Holmes made an exception to his general embrace of judicial restraint. He strongly favored protection of free speech. Consider these heroic words: "But when men have realized that time has upset many fighting faiths, they may come to believe even more than they believe the very foundations of their own conduct that the ultimate good desired is better reached by free trade in ideas—that the best test of truth is the power of the thought to get itself accepted in the competition of the market, and that truth is the only ground upon which their wishes safely can be carried out. That, at any rate, is the theory of our Constitution."[4]

In insisting on judicial protection of freedom of speech, Holmes was a Hero, not a Soldier, apparently because he believed that free speech was a precondition for the democratic process itself. But his heroism was essentially limited to that context.

There are many distinguished academic defenses of the Soldier. Writing at the turn of the twentieth century, Harvard law professor James Bradley Thayer was a great and highly influential advocate of judicial deference to the outcomes of political processes. He is the most important early defender of the soldierly conception of the judicial role. In Thayer's view, the Supreme Court should not invalidate legislation unless the violation of the Constitution's text is unmistakably clear and entirely unambiguous. Thayer's position was a radical one, and it would have major consequences. The text of the Constitution is often ambiguous, and if courts must uphold legislation whenever they find ambiguity, they will uphold almost everything. What, exactly, counts as "the freedom of speech"? What does it mean to violate the right to "due process of law"? Thayer would allow the elected branches of government to do whatever they want whenever the Constitution is ambiguous, and so his view would lead to a passive, soldierly Court.

Because the Constitution does not unambiguously forbid racial segregation, even *Brown v. Board of Education* would be hard to defend. True, the Constitution forbids states from denying people "the equal protection of the laws," but it is hardly clear that racial segregation counts as such a denial. (I hasten to add that I think that *Brown* was rightly decided; the only point is that the consistent Soldier would have to dissent.) Sex discrimination would certainly be permissible, and states could forbid married couples from having access to contraceptives. Note as well that there are many possible interpretations of the words "the freedom of speech." Some people believe that the words are directed only at prior restraint (as, for example, through a licensing scheme for speakers) and do not forbid subsequent punishment of speech (as, for example, through criminal penalties). For this reason,

Thayer's position would lead to a narrow understanding of the free speech principle. It would almost certainly allow state governments to compel school prayer and to require departures from the principle of one person, one vote.

It is true that even if we are inclined to agree with Thayer, we might think that what matters is not merely the text of the Constitution, but the original understanding of the meaning of the text, and hence that judges should be free to invalidate legislation if it clearly violates the original understanding. If so, judges would have more occasions to be heroic. But since the original understanding is itself often ambiguous, an originalist who agrees with Thayer would have to accept almost all, and possibly all, of these results.

Law professor Adrian Vermeule is the most sophisticated contemporary proponent of soldiering, with his careful argument in favor of judicial deference to the outcomes of political processes.[5] Judge J. Harvie Wilkinson has taken essentially the same position, seeking to reduce the role of the judiciary, and judge-made constitutional law, in American life.

There are many other proponents of soldiering. Some people challenge judicial review altogether; they do not believe that courts should have the authority to strike down legislation at all. Others stress the ultimate sovereignty of We the People; they believe that at least if they make their views clear, the People, and not the judges, are entitled to have the final say. Still others embrace populist accounts of constitutional law; they argue that the meaning of the Constitution is, and should be, a product of what the public thinks at any moment in time, at least on questions of high principle. On a populist account, the Court should be tracking public opinion, at least if it is deliberative and considered. Those who hold these views are likely to endorse the Persona of the Soldier, at least to some degree.

To their admirers, Soldiers count as heroic, because they adopt the proper role and respect the limited place of the judiciary in the constitutional system. While Soldiers can unquestionably be seen as heroic, they are not Heroes. They do not care whether they are on the wrong side of history, and they certainly do not stand athwart anything and yell "Stop." To Soldiers, Heroes suffer from hubris. Because Soldiers do not want courts to engage in social reform, and because they defer to the political process, Heroes tend to see Soldiers as timid and weak, even cowardly—as abdicating and refusing to assume their constitutionally assigned functions.

As with heroism, so with soldiering: there are Equal Protection Soldiers, Due Process Soldiers, Commerce Clause Soldiers, Second Amendment Soldiers, Article II, Soldiers, Fourth Amendment Soldiers, Takings Soldiers, Standing Soldiers, and many more. A judge might endorse soldiering with respect to one provision but reject it with respect to others, and again this pattern is common. If a court embraces heroism in some domains, it is likely to embrace soldiering in others. There is no logical necessity here; some people (like Thayer and Vermeule) do want soldiering in all contexts. But the phenomenon of *selective heroism and soldiering* is unmistakable and familiar, with (for example) both the Warren Court and the *Lochner* Court showing precisely that pattern.

Second-Order Soldiers

To this general account of the Soldier, there is an important qualification. While soldiering as I understand it is associated with judicial deference to the political process, and while I am treating Holmes as the iconic Soldier, other judges, with positions distinctly different from that of Holmes, can and do claim the mantle of Soldier as well. Consider originalists, such as Justices Clarence Thomas, Antonin Scalia, and Hugo Black, who seek to follow We the People, and to track the judgments of those who ratified the founding document. To that extent, they too can plausibly be described as Soldiers. Indeed, a form of soldiering is built into their self-presentation, and it is a large part of what gives originalism its intuitive appeal. They too contend that they are simply following orders, not offering moral readings or venturing their own personal accounts of what the Constitution requires. Justice Scalia believes in a "rock-solid, unchanging" Constitution, and insofar as he claims to be following the People's orders, he is certainly acting as a Soldier. Voting to uphold bans on same-sex marriage, Justice Scalia emphasizes the need to defer to the political process and to democracy itself.

At the same time, Soldiers of this kind are entirely willing to invalidate the actions of the federal government or of the states. To the extent that this is so, it is because they are Soldiers, not in spite of that fact. Consider these words from Justice Scalia, in his soldierly opinion for the Court, holding that the Second Amendment establishes an individual right: "Constitutional rights are enshrined with the scope they were understood to have when the people adopted them, whether or not future legislatures or (yes) even future judges think that scope too broad."[6]

We should therefore distinguish between first-order Soldiers, who defer to the judgments of the political process, and second-order Soldiers, who can in a sense count as Hero-Soldiers, willing to trump those judgments when the original public meaning of the Constitution so requires. In fact, many judges present themselves as second-order Soldiers, even if they reject originalism. They contend that they are merely following the Constitution, and adhering to its mandates, even if the result is to strike down legislation.

We can go further. Soldiering is the most fundamental and enduring part of the judicial self-presentation and even of judges' self-understanding. When judges seek to be confirmed, they insist that they are Soldiers, simply following the rules. They say that they "will just follow the law." Because the rules and the law are often vague and ambiguous, especially when the Supreme Court gets involved, that's a bit of a cheat, even a fraud; you can't just follow the law when there is no law to follow. But it is nonetheless revealing that judges (and judicial nominees) like to return to the mantra of fidelity to law. In referring to Soldiers, I shall be speaking of the first-order variety unless otherwise indicated.

MINIMALISTS

Some judges are neither Heroes nor Soldiers but Minimalists, in the sense that they favor small, cautious steps, building incrementally on the decisions and practices of the past. Unlike Heroes, who celebrate ambitious accounts of liberty and equality or of the Constitution's structural provisions, those who adopt the minimalist Persona emphasize the limits of large-scale theories. They emphasize that human beings, and judges in particular, have a limited stock of reason. They embrace the idea of humility. They use that idea not as a basis for soldiering, but as a reason for small steps.

In dealing with cases involving basic rights, Minimalists insist on two different points. First, they do not want to embrace any kind of foundational theory. They do not want to adopt large accounts of liberty or property. They prefer *shallowness to depth*. They tend to argue for careful attention not to abstractions but to traditions, understood at a level of concreteness. Consider the words of the great social theorist Edmund Burke, an inspiration for Minimalists of all kinds, who challenged the primacy of abstract theories: "And first of all, the science of jurisprudence, the pride of the human intellect, which, with all its defects, redundancies, and errors, is the collected reason of ages, combining the principles of original justice with the infinite variety of human concerns, as a heap of old exploded errors, would no longer be studied. Personal self-sufficiency and arrogance (the certain attendants upon all those who have never experienced a wisdom greater than their own) would usurp the tribunal."[7]

Second, Minimalists favor narrow rulings, focused on the facts of particular cases. They want courts to focus on the specific issues before them. They prefer *narrowness to width*. When sitting on the court of appeals, Chief Justice Roberts captured this preference with an aphoristic summary of the minimalist position in constitutional law: "If it is not necessary to decide more, it is necessary not to decide more."

In many of his opinions, Roberts has followed this position, embracing narrow rulings that leave many questions undecided. Case-by-case adjudication is part of the minimalist creed.

The most committed Minimalists will choose minimalism in all or almost all contexts. But some judges might be more cautious (and in a sense minimalist) with respect to minimalism itself, insisting that the decision whether to be minimalist is best resolved case-by-case. (I will return to this point in chapters 3 and 4.) And in arguing against theoretical ambition and in favor of narrowness, a judge might endorse minimalism with respect to one constitutional provision but reject it with respect to others. We can imagine judges who are separation-of-powers Minimalists but free speech Heroes. Indeed, that approach might appeal to judges in principle (see chapter 3 for details).

With their modesty and humility, Minimalists might seem to be close cousins of those Soldiers who are reluctant to invalidate legislation, and alliances are certainly possible between the two Personae. But the two are fundamentally different breeds. Minimalists do not purport to be following anyone's orders or will. They acknowledge and even insist that judges exercise discretion. They think that Soldiers are often frauds, because they disguise the role of their own judgments. To Minimalists, that fact poses a serious problem. Minimalists claim that it is best for judges to exercise their discretion in a way that brackets foundational questions and that ensures small, incremental steps from the status quo. They believe that judges should speak softly and carry a small stick.

Notwithstanding this point, some Heroes do present themselves as Minimalists, contending that a heroic decision is merely an incremental step. We can certainly imagine at least mildly heroic Minimalists, who are genuinely committed to incrementalism and who reject the largest theories, but who are nonetheless willing to wield judicial power so as to invalidate legislation. On some occasions, Minimalists might be counted as Heroes as I have used the term, though of a relatively modest variety. When the Court struck down the ban on same-sex

CONSTITUTIONAL PERSONAE

sodomy in *Lawrence v. Texas*, it proceeded in a relatively minimalist fashion, focusing on the problem at hand without venturing into
unnecessary territory by saying a lot more about sexual privacy or the
rights of gays and lesbians.

Because of his enthusiasm for tradition, his commitment to
case-by-case judgment, and his skepticism about large-scale theories,
Justice Felix Frankfurter can be seen as an iconic Minimalist. Justice
John Marshall Harlan, a conservative on the Warren Court, falls in
the same category, and in some ways, he may be the most minimalist
justice of all. Justice Sandra Day O'Connor showed strong minimalist
inclinations, especially insofar as she liked to focus narrowly on the
facts of particular cases. Chief Justice Roberts has written a number of
minimalist opinions, and hence on prominent occasions, he appears to
be a self-conscious Minimalist. Justice Ruth Bader Ginsburg can also
be counted as a Minimalist, in the sense that she emphasizes the need
to focus carefully on both facts and precedents.

From this catalog, it should be clear that no less than Heroes and
Soldiers, Minimalists come in different shapes and sizes. All of them
prize narrow, theoretically unambitious rulings, but they may well
disagree with one another about which kind of narrow, unambitious
ruling is best. Minimalism is not a complete theory of the judicial role.
As we shall see in chapter 3, some Minimalists emphasize tradition,
and the importance of respecting it, whereas others demand reasons for
public practices and think that traditions may be based on prejudice or
power, and hence unworthy of respect.

MUTES

While Minimalists favor narrow and unambitious rulings, Mutes prefer to say nothing at all. Of course no judge can be a consistent or
frequent Mute, and for that reason, Mutes are infrequent players in the

constitutional drama. But whenever fundamental issues are at stake, the Persona of the Mute will have its attractions.

For example, Mutes are drawn to the important and time-honored strategy of "constitutional avoidance," by which justices resolve cases without deciding constitutional questions. Often justices work hard to avoid such questions, and to remain silent on them, by interpreting statutes in such a way as to make it unnecessary to speak to them. They might say, for example, that a congressional enactment that appears to intrude on freedom of speech does no such thing, because the enactment is ambiguous, and can be interpreted not to intrude on freedom in any way. In technical terms, judges favor interpretations that avoid constitutional doubts—and that therefore ensure a discreet silence on the most fundamental issues.

Mutes are also attracted to doctrines of "justiciability," which prevent courts from deciding cases and thus limit the reach of judicial authority, permitting or requiring courts to say nothing at all. Judges might, for example, rule that a controversy is not "ripe" for resolution, or that the complaining party lacks standing, or that the case has become moot. In addition, judges cannot issue advisory opinions, and this prohibition often enables them to be silent.

The Court also has control over its own jurisdiction, and it can decide that some cases ought not to be decided (now, or yet), even if those cases are quite important, and even if the lower courts are divided. It might decide not to decide on the ground that the nation is severely split on some controversial issue (until recently, same-sex marriage was an example), and it does not want to weigh in until the timing is right. Mutes are enthusiastic about the idea that the Court should often refuse to resolve hotly disputed issues, on which the nation is divided. With his enthusiastic embrace of "the passive virtues," through which the Court declines to rule on the merits, Yale law professor Alexander Bickel was the great theorist of constitutional muteness.[8] Bickel thought that being passive could be virtuous, because it allowed the American public to continue to discuss and debate, and because it did not prematurely insert the judges into the process.

Bickel's own approach emphasizes the strategic and prudential importance of silence, especially on large questions of basic morality that split nations. Within families, it is sometimes a good idea not to bring the hardest questions out into the open, at least not at the wrong time. Return in this light to the question of same-sex marriage. For Bickel, justices are entitled to be strategists; they can silence themselves for a period and then strike when the timing is best, in the sense that society is prepared to listen to them and to acquiesce. Bickel also believed that prudence is an important judicial virtue, and that prudent people know when to shut up. Bickel insisted that the Court must be principled (always), but he also emphasized that no society could afford to be principle-ridden. By principled, he did not mean that the Court should follow the original understanding of the Constitution; Bickel was no originalist. He meant to say that the Constitution required the Court to give its own principled content to its majestic phrases. Bickel saw the justices as giving moral readings to the founding document, and for that reason, he had a great deal of sympathy for Heroes. But he believed that there was grave tension between the idea of judicial Heroes, whether or not they were right, and the basic requirements of a self-governing society. For this reason, the justices must often silence themselves, even if the moral question is clear.

With respect to issues of racial justice in the 1950s and 1960s, for example, Bickel believed that the Court could not insist on immediate and full implementation of a principle of equality. It had to wait until the nation was ready for it. A defender of the ban on school segregation, Bickel favored silence on the question of whether states could ban racial intermarriage. Of course he had no enthusiasm for such bans as such. But when the Court was engaged in a series of intense constitutional controversies, many of them involving segregation, he believed that it was appropriate for the Court to stay its hand. In Bickel's account, premature judicial engagement could have had a range of harmful consequences for both the nation and the Court, producing backlash, diminishing the Court's limited capital, and as a result, potentially endangering the very goals of racial equality that the Court sought to promote.

To defend his account of muteness, Bickel invoked the example of Abraham Lincoln, who always insisted that slavery was morally unacceptable, but who believed that in deciding when and how to eliminate it, a degree of prudence, and self-silencing, was entirely legitimate, indeed indispensable. In an important sense, Lincoln was an early advocate of muteness in the political domain. In Lincoln's view, the feeling of "the great mass of white people" would not permit immediate abolition of slavery. In his most striking formulation, Lincoln declared: "Whether this feeling accords with justice and sound judgment, is not the sole question, if indeed, it is any part of it. A universal feeling, whether well or ill-founded, can not be safely disregarded." Bickel thought that the Court should follow Lincoln's example. For Bickel, the Mute was an honorable and even heroic figure.

Other people are drawn to muteness on grounds of humility—which is, in my view, the most important point in favor of self-silencing in law (and politics as well). Judges should know that there is a great deal that they do not know. Suppose, for example, that they are faced with a genuinely hard question about surveillance designed to protect national security, or about regulation of some new technology. When judges lack relevant knowledge—of facts or values—it might be best to say nothing at all. Of course a degree of humility is a defining characteristic of the Minimalist, who is acutely aware of his own limitations. But those very limitations might lead judges to decline to speak to certain controversies, at least until they receive more information. Bickel stressed strategic and prudential considerations, but for many Mutes, the real issue is that they are acutely aware of their own limitations and are not at all sure that their impressions and inclinations are right. That awareness might extend to the content of basic rights; it might be particularly important in the context of disputes over national security, where the stakes are high and judges are rarely specialists. When the nation is threatened, many judges will be interested in the claims of silence.

Still other people favor muteness on more distinctly legal grounds, emphasizing what they regard as the restrictions of Article III of the Constitution. In their (soldierly) view, justices have no business thinking in terms of strategy or prudence. The real point, and the only important one, is that the Constitution often *requires* the justices to say nothing at all, because they cannot act unless there is a "case" or "controversy." We can therefore identify Mute Soldiers, who maintain silence not for strategic or prudential reasons, but because of what they see as the commands of the Constitution itself.

Suppose, for example, that members of Congress are seeking to sue the president to require him to act in accordance with the law as they understand it. (The House of Representatives famously, or notoriously, authorized such a suit against President Barack Obama in 2014.) Judges might well refuse to hear the case, and thus remain mute, on the ground that the Constitution does not allow members of Congress to sue the president, even if they are right to think that he acted unlawfully. The problem is not that the president did in fact obey the law. The problem is that the Constitution does not allow courts to resolve the question. Here yet again, a judge might endorse muteness with respect to one provision (or even controversy), but reject it with respect to others.

As a prominent example of muteness, consider *Naim v. Naim*, in which the Court declined to pronounce on the constitutionality of restrictions on racial intermarriage. *Naim v. Naim* may well be history's most important illustration of muteness in action. The Court refused to rule on a form of racial discrimination that was unquestionably invidious and essentially impossible to defend on constitutional grounds. But as I have noted, Bickel had a great deal of sympathy for the Court's silence. If its muteness was defensible on grounds of strategy and prudence, it was because the Court had already engaged the nation on a series of important civil rights and civil liberties issues, above all segregation, and the engagement was splitting the nation, and in some ways threatening to tear it apart. For that reason, the time was not right to tackle the issue of miscegenation.

In short, the Court was both conserving its political capital and giving the democratic process some extra space. Or consider *Poe v. Ulman*, in which the Court declined to review a Connecticut law forbidding the sale and use of contraceptives. That decision not to decide is another prominent illustration of muteness. In view of the highly controversial character of that question, the Court did not want to resolve it in 1961 (though it elected to do so in 1965, when it struck down the Connecticut law).

In *Hollingsworth v. Perry*, the Court invoked the doctrine of standing to dismiss a challenge to a California law banning recognition of same-sex marriage. ("Standing" requires people to have an "injury in fact" if they seek to invoke the authority of the courts; in *Hollingsworth*, the Court said that the plaintiffs lacked standing.) That decision is the twenty-first century's best example of muteness. On same-sex marriage, the Court elected to stay silent (though of course not for long).

On one view, of course, the constitutional materials simply prohibited the Court from hearing the case. The issue of standing is highly technical, but perhaps we could understand the case as one in which Soldiers decided to be Mutes, because muteness is just what the Constitution required them to be. It seems far more sensible, however, to suggest that at least some of the justices did not *want* to address the issue at that time. Instead they sought to allow democratic debate to continue and hoped for a continued evolution in social values. Perhaps some such justices were displaying the virtue of prudence. Perhaps some were behaving strategically. Perhaps some believed that they were not themselves sufficiently clear on how to resolve the question. True Soldiers would want, of course, to leave the issue at that, allowing citizens, and not courts, to resolve the question of same-sex marriage. But some Mutes, in this and other contexts, have been biding their time.

We should be able to see that Minimalists and Mutes belong in the same family, and that the difference between them can be taken as one of degree. They are cousins, not adversaries, and they have similar motivations. Narrowness ensures a degree of muteness; the same is true of shallowness. Minimalists want to be mute on many things. The difference between the two Personae—and it is an important one—is that Mutes hope to say nothing at all.

DUELING PERSONAE

It is easy to find examples of the Personae in action. Many constitutional disputes, and all of the large ones, pit them directly against one another. Such disputes are often illuminatingly seen as stylized debates among the four Personae, with one or another judge assuming a particular role, depending on the issue and the context.

In the Abstract

In those disputes, the Hero might invoke a large-scale understanding of equality or liberty (consider the right to free speech), or perhaps of the limits on federal power under the Constituton's Article I (recall the dispute over the Affordable Care Act). The Soldier responds that courts should defer to the outcomes of the political process unless the constitutional infirmity is quite clear—and concludes that it is not. In this way, the Soldier accuses the Hero of arrogance or hubris, a willingness to impose a particular vision of the Constitution on the nation as a whole. To the Soldier, the Hero is a tyrant.

The Hero responds, implicitly or explicitly, that the Soldier is lawless, willing to disregard clear constitutional constraints on government power, and even to insult the power of judicial review, perhaps because what the Hero sees as the Soldier's unduly narrow conception of liberty or equality. The Hero likes to say to the Soldier, "If the Constitution means anything, it means that the government cannot do *this!*" To the Hero, the Soldier is a coward, even a kind of infidel. The Hero believes that the Soldier is not respecting liberty or equality and is defying our constitutional traditions. The Hero asks a question: *What's a Constitution for, if not to check the majority?*

The Minimalist rejects both positions. Like the Soldier, he accuses the Hero of hubris. But he contends that the Soldier is arrogant in his own way, insofar as he adopts a large-scale posture of deference (which the Minimalist regards as grounded in the Soldier's own theory, or the Soldier's favored abstraction of some kind). For the Minimalist, the Soldier is not really humble; he has adopted a large abstraction ("defer to the political process") and used it as a kind of all-purpose response to serious constitutional disputes. The Minimalist asks the Soldier: Aren't you in the grip of a big theory of your own? And isn't that theory a bit silly, even absurd? Do you really want to uphold school segregation and discrimination on the basis of sex? To allow restrictions on freedom of speech and freedom of religion?

Against both the Hero and the Soldier, the Minimalist insists on the importance of avoiding large, abstract pronouncements and the value of engaging carefully with the particular facts. The Minimalist argues on behalf of adhering to social traditions and judicial precedents. He sees Heroes and Soldiers as insufficiently respectful of either.

If the Hero responds to the Minimalist at all, he will insist that the Constitution does identify a general principle, that it is legitimate and important to identify it, and that clarity in the law is far preferable to case-by-case meandering and obscurantism. To the Hero, the

Minimalist does not believe in the rule of law. The Hero will insist that there is nothing arrogant in saying that the Constitution forbids segregation, safeguards the right to dissent, limits national power, or protects an individual's right to possess firearms. The subtext of the heroic response will be that the Minimalist is fearful—and even worse, that he is fearful of what justice, or the law, plainly requires. The Hero also objects that the Minimalist leaves too many issues undecided and uncertain, making it impossible for people to know what the law is.

For his part, the Soldier will regard the Minimalist as a temporizer, unwilling to show the proper respect for the democratic branches and leaving a degree of chaos for lower courts to sort out. Where the Minimalist sees prudence, the Soldier sees a distinctive kind of arrogance, captured in a foolish belief that it is sensible to issue opinions that are shallow and narrow. The Soldier complains of what he sees as the Soldier's inexplicable focus on particular cases, as opposed to what is plainly justified: a willingness to adopt a broad principle in favor of deference. The Soldier believes that a posture of deference is what principle, and the Constitution, require, and that humility is best exemplified with that posture, rather than with case-by-case maneuvering.

The Mute will object to the Hero and the Soldier on grounds similar to those invoked by the Minimalist—but a bit more extreme. To the Mute, the proper course is to allow the democratic process to play itself out. Judges ought not to be taking sides, especially when society is divided or in the midst of some kind of moral evolution. Both invalidation and validation are unacceptable.

For the Mute, invalidation is worst of all, because it disables self-government. But judicial validation is also troublesome in light of its legitimating or expressive effect in the very domain that people are actively debating. Mutes are especially troubled by the expressive effect of constitutional rulings. When the Court rules that some practice is constitutional, many people understand the Court as taking sides by saying that the practice is morally acceptable. That is unfortunate, a terrible misreading of what a constitutional ruling is actually about, because judges can and do uphold practices that they abhor. But the misunderstanding is hard to avoid. If, for example, the Court had upheld a ban on racial intermarriage in the 1960s, many people would have taken it to have placed its imprimatur on a morally unacceptable and racist practice—as if the justices were announcing that the practice was unobjectionable. (Imagine that the Court had upheld bans on same-sex marriage in, say, 2005.) To the Mute, it is far better for the Court to say nothing than to say that such a practice is constitutionally permissible. To be sure, the Mute is a lot more sympathetic to the Minimalist than to the Hero or the Soldier, but she believes that it is simpler and cleaner to stay out of the area entirely rather than to take an incremental step.

Of course the Hero has no patience for the Mute, who (in the Hero's view) is abdicating the judicial role and allowing the Constitution to be ignored in the process. The Soldier insists that the Mute is wrong to stay silent when judges might instead clarify that the issue is for the political process to resolve. To Heroes and Soldiers, silence is anything but golden. The Minimalist and the Mute have overlapping concerns, but the Minimalist tends to believe that a small, incremental step is highly desirable, because it moves the ball in the preferred direction. In the Minimalist's view, the Mute is too coy by half.

On the Ground

We can see these kinds of disputes in countless areas. As I have emphasized, no judge consistently adopts a particular Persona, but for purposes of exposition, it will be useful to bracket that point and ask how those who assume a particular Persona, in particular cases, will engage with one another. It should be clear that a judge who is a Hero in one area (say, Justice Scalia in affirmative action cases, where he would invalidate essentially all such programs) might be a Soldier in another

[27]

(say, Justice Scalia in abortion cases, where he would uphold essentially all restrictions).

For one illustration, consider academic and judicial debates over the constitutionality of restrictions on same-sex marriage. Heroes have long insisted that such restrictions are unacceptable; they would enlist the equal protection clause in support of that conclusion. Citing the example of *Brown*, and even more the heroic decision in *Loving v. Virginia* (the best-named case in all of constitutional law, striking down bans on racial intermarriage), many people have argued in this direction. In their view, restrictions on same-sex marriage intrude on a fundamental liberty and reflect unconstitutional "animus" against gays and lesbians. Of course, a majority of the Court adopted the heroic Personae in 2015.

By contrast, Soldiers would defer to the political process, arguing that there is nothing in the Constitution to forbid such restrictions and saying, in Justice Scalia's words, "the Constitution neither requires nor forbids our society to approve of same-sex marriage, much as it neither requires nor forbids us to approve of no-fault divorce, polygamy, or the consumption of alcohol."

At least if they are not prepared to defer to traditions, Minimalists would favor narrow, incompletely theorized decisions, leaving the most fundamental questions for another day. In 2012, for example, the Department of Justice urged the Court to take a broadly minimalist approach, suggesting that the justices should decline to resolve the largest questions about same-sex marriage and should rule more narrowly that those states that have recognized same-sex civil unions cannot be permitted to deny those unions the label of "marriage." Under this approach, the Court would bracket (if it could) the question whether states could refuse to recognize same-sex marriages altogether. For their part, Mutes would want the justices to use doctrines of justiciability to stay entirely out of this domain; we have seen that the Court's use of standing in *Hollingsworth* is a conspicuous example of the triumph of the Persona of the Mute. For example, Mutes have wanted the Court to use its power over its own jurisdiction to decline to review lower-court rulings on the topic.

The same Personae can be found in many other constitutional disputes. *Roe v. Wade*, protecting the right to choose abortion, is emphatically heroic, and indeed it is one of the most heroic decisions of the last fifty years—and roundly criticized for that reason. Many of those who think the decision was wrong claim the mantle of Soldiers and insist that the Constitution does not speak to the issue and that the Court should have allowed the states to regulate abortion as they saw fit. Justices Scalia and Thomas, for example, think that in the area of abortion, the Constitution requires soldiering. Many people who do not agree with their general approach think that on this particular question, they are essentially right. They might believe that the question whether fetal life should be protected, even at the earliest stages, is a genuinely difficult one, and that states should be allowed to resolve the moral question as they like.

By contrast, Minimalists wish the *Roe* Court had ruled narrowly—not by protecting a broad right to choose abortion but by striking down bans on abortion in cases of rape and incest, or perhaps by saying that laws that restrict abortion cannot be unduly vague. Embracing minimalism, Justice Ginsburg has argued that the Court should have proceeded on a path of this kind, emphasizing narrowness. Of course Mutes believe that it would have been better if the Court had endeavored not to speak to the abortion question at all. Especially illuminating debates have occurred in this domain, with Heroes contending that women have a right to choose as they see fit, and Soldiers, Minimalists, and Mutes offering their predictable counterarguments.

Or consider *Citizens United*, protecting the right of corporations to spend on political campaigns. That decision is emphatically heroic, with its strong claims about freedom of speech and its connection with campaign expenditures. Sharply critical of that decision, Soldiers, Minimalists, and Mutes can easily be found in debates over campaign finance legislation. In that area, some of the most intense disputes are between Heroes (including Justices Scalia and Thomas), who want to take an especially strong stand against restrictions on the use of money in campaigns, and Minimalists (such as Justice O'Connor), who have sought to build cautiously on current law. Of course there have also been Soldiers, such as Justices John Paul Stevens and Thurgood Marshall, who insist that Congress should be allowed broad discretion to restrict the expenditure of money for political purposes. In their view, the Constitution does not have all that much to say about that question, and We the People, acting through the democratic process, should generally be allowed to act if the goal is to avoid corruption or to ensure that economic inequalities are not translated into political equalities. For this reason, courts should keep their hands off.

Heroes, prominently including Justices Scalia and Thomas, wanted to invalidate the Affordable Care Act, while Soldiers wanted to uphold it. Here yet again, Mutes would avoid the question and would hope that the Court would not address the constitutional questions at all. For their part, Minimalists would seek to rule as narrowly as possible, avoiding big pronouncements about congressional power—perhaps by invalidating the act on narrow grounds, and more likely by upholding it on such grounds. Or consider the great 2014 debate over the constitutionality of recess appointments by the president, by which the chief executive avoids the Senate confirmation process by installing his own nominees while the Senate is on "recess." The scope of the president's power to make such appointments has long been disputed, with modern (and not-so-modern) presidents asserting far broader authority than many senators have been comfortable with. Fans of judicial Heroes wanted the Court to rule firmly against such practices, and during the Obama administration, many Republicans endorsed heroism. Mutes would of course have stayed out of the controversy altogether. By contrast, Minimalists wanted the Court to rule more narrowly, and with careful reference to traditions. Led by Justice Breyer, Minimalists prevailed (but by a 5–4 vote and so barely).

HISTORY'S LESSONS

Some of these disagreements are influenced by a reading of history and by an understanding of the lesson of canonical examples and counter-examples. When have the Court's decisions been most admirable, and when has it embarrassed or even disgraced itself? Evaluations of the Personae are often a product of the answer to that question.

I have noted that Heroes tend to invoke *Brown*, seeing it as iconic; we have seen that many Heroes do not want to be on the wrong side of history. For such Heroes, *New York Times v. Sullivan*, protecting free speech in the face of libel laws, and *Reynolds v. Sims*, establishing a rule of one person, one vote, are iconic too. For many Heroes, *Lawrence v. Texas*, striking down a criminal ban on sexual acts between people of the same gender, is an excellent example of an iconic decision (though it can also be characterized as minimalist insofar as it is relatively narrow).

For many Heroes, prominent anti-icons—symbols of what must be avoided—include *Plessy v. Ferguson*, upholding racial segregation and thus allowing a form of apartheid in the United States (for many decades); *Korematsu v. United States*, upholding the internment of Japanese Americans during World War II and thus symbolizing the Supreme Court's willingness to authorize the government's incorporation of racial prejudice; and *Bowers v. Hardwick*, upholding a criminal ban on sexual acts between people of the same gender (and overruled in *Lawrence*). Most Heroes really do not want to write or join another *Plessy*, and they certainly do not want to replicate the experience in *Korematsu* or *Bowers*. Concerned about what they see as judicial abdication during wartime, many Heroes regard *Korematsu* in particular as an example of what goes wrong when judges operate as Soldiers, deferring to a nation that fails to respect the dignity of many of its members. In their view, *Korematsu* is a moral and legal disgrace, and it shows how Soldiers can go badly wrong.

Other Heroes, with different substantive (and especially conservative or libertarian) orientations, single out the 1942 decision *Wickard v. Filburn* as an anti-icon. In that case, the Court greatly expanded the power of the national government, seeming to stretch the meaning of the Constitution's commerce clause in such a way as to give Congress something akin to broad and general authority to regulate the economy—even when effects on interstate commerce are far from clear. For similar reasons, some conservative Heroes and Hero-worshippers reject and deplore *NFIB v. Sebelius*, upholding the Affordable Care Act, and *United States v. Carolene Products*, where the Court announced a general presumption in favor of upholding economic regulation. To the critics, the problem with these decisions is that they suggest a degree of soldierly deference to legislation that is, in their view, plainly illegitimate. Arguing for heroism, many conservatives and libertarians contend that in these and related cases, the Court has ignored the plain meaning of the Constitution. In such areas, the tension between Heroes and Soldiers is especially acute.

For their part, Soldiers tend to see *Dred Scott*, in which the Court exercised its authority so as to entrench the institution of slavery, as the worst decision in all of the anticanon. They also focus on, and abhor, *Lochner v. New York*, in which the Court struck down maximum hour laws. They are acutely aware of, and they enthusiastically embrace, Justice Holmes's cautionary notes about the hazards of reading any particular moral or political theory into the Constitution. (They reject both conservative and progressive approaches for that reason.) Many Soldiers object to *Miranda v. Arizona*, protecting the rights of criminal defendants, which they regard as a form of lawless heroism. A lot of Soldiers believe that *Roe v. Wade* is a more recent incarnation of *Lochner*—and they invoke what they see as the sad tale of *Roe* as a reason for deference to political processes.

Soldiers celebrate *West Coast Hotel v. Parrish*, in which the Court abandoned its aggressive posture against economic legislation in the

New Deal and emphasized the need for judicial deference in the economic realm. In their view, *West Coast Hotel* is iconic (and good). They think the same for *Wickard*, because of its deferential approach to congressional power under the commerce clause, and also *Katzenbach v. Morgan*, where the Court endorsed the idea of broad judicial deference to exercise of congressional power to protect individual rights under the Fourteenth Amendment.

It is important to acknowledge, however, that second-order Soldiers—above all originalists, who think that they must follow the Constitution's original meaning—understand *Lochner*, *Roe*, and *Miranda* as wrong not merely or even mostly because they invalidated the outcomes of democratic processes, but because they did so without a sufficient warrant in the original meaning of the Constitution. These kinds of Soldiers reject *Lochner* and *Roe*. But some of them, focused on the original understanding, are perfectly willing to strike down limits on the individual right to possess firearms, to invoke the limited nature of the Commerce Power to strike down the Affordable Care Act, and generally to reinvigorate restrictions on the power of the national government. Many contemporary libertarians claim that their views are supported by the original understanding; they claim to be Soldiers.

Some Minimalists are fully prepared to celebrate the Court's sex discrimination cases, in which the Court did not rule broadly all at once, but instead proceeded narrowly and cautiously toward a principle of sex equality. For those (progressive) Minimalists, the sex discrimination cases are iconic, because the Court chose to move slowly and case-by-case. Minimalists tend to see *Roe* as objectionable not because it took steps to protect the right to choose, but because of its heroism, embodied in a broad, ambitious ruling, going well beyond what was necessary to decide the case. In this sense, *Roe* is a minimalist anti-icon. As noted, *Naim v. Naim* occupies pride of place in the canon of muteness—and the 5–4 decision in *Hollingsworth v. Perry*, understood as an exercise of the passive virtues, has joined it.

PERSONAE AS (MERE) LITERARY DEVICES?

One way to understand the Personae is as rhetorical or literary devices. On this understanding, the Soldier (for example) has a characteristic rhetorical strategy, which is to say, "I am compelled to do X, even though I might like to do Y." This strategy might be, and is, used both by first-order and second-order Soldiers. Sometimes the rhetoric matches reality. The Soldier might be following orders. But sometimes the rhetoric is a fraud.

The equal protection clause could, for example, be construed to permit or to forbid affirmative action programs—or even to require them. The text and history are unclear. (In fact, the better view is probably that on the original understanding, the equal protection clause allows affirmative action.) If Soldiers vote to forbid such programs, and claim to be compelled to do so, their rhetoric is a mask for an exercise of discretion. And indeed, some second-order Soldiers write as if they had no choice but to strike down affirmative action programs. That's false. Unfortunately, many Soldiers are willing to don rhetorical masks.

Something similar could be said about some Minimalists, who like to say that they are building narrowly on precedent, even if what they are doing is a novelty or a substantial departure, or plausibly characterized as a form of heroism. In the area of campaign finance, a judge who is a Hero—in the sense of believing in strong free speech safeguards, dooming regulation—might purport to follow precedent, and to be ruling narrowly and modestly, where the real consequence is across-the-board invalidation, or something close to it.

To be sure, it is not possible to disguise or feign muteness, but a judge might adopt the Persona of the Mute not because of a principled commitment to a form of soldiering (as in the view that Article III requires muteness), but as a rhetorical gambit designed as part of "the long game." A judge who wants to require all states to respect same-sex marriage might maintain silence in 2005 or 2008 or 2012, but plan to speak clearly when the time is right. 2015, as it turned out. On this view, the analysis of Constitutional Personae might be properly regarded as belonging to the study of judicial politics or even law and literature.

This view is not exactly wrong, and much can be learned by examining the Constitutional Personae in this light. But I am understanding them quite differently here. I suggest that we should see the Personae not as a matter of judicial politics or rhetoric, but instead as a reflection of how different judges actually understand their jobs, and of how they perform those jobs in different contexts. When scholars defend the moral reading of the Constitution (and thus embrace heroism), they are not adopting a mere rhetorical stance; the same is true of judges who essentially attempt moral readings. And when judges operate as Soldiers, it may well be because that Persona captures their understanding of their appropriate role.

PERSONAE AND THEORIES OF INTERPRETATION

It is natural to wonder about the relationship between the Constitutional Personae and standard theories of constitutional interpretation. We can already glimpse the basic answer, which is that the standard theories can lead to adoption of one or another of the Personae, depending on the occasion. The words "depending on the occasion" are important. As we shall see, any one of the Personae can fall out of a given theory of interpretation. What matters is exactly when it does so, and here the relevant theory is critical. It would make no sense to adopt a Persona in the abstract; a Persona is defensible only if it follows from the appropriate approach to the Constitution.

Theories First, Persona Second?

Suppose that judges embrace originalism and insist that the founding document must be construed to fit with the original meaning. (We will encounter some complexities in chapter 2.) Such judges would be Mutes when the original understanding of Article III so requires. But they would be Hero-Soldiers if (say) the original understanding of the Commerce Clause or the Fourteenth Amendment calls for invalidation of the Affordable Care Act or affirmative action programs. And they would become Soldiers if the original understanding of the Fourteenth Amendment requires them to uphold restrictions on same-sex marriage. Originalism requires judges to adopt the particular Persona that follows from the Constitution's original meaning.

Suppose, by contrast, that judges believe that the Constitution should be construed so as to promote democratic self-government (as Justice Breyer has urged) and thus seek to understand the Constitution in such a way as to improve democratic processes. If so, they might be Heroes on free speech and voting rights (to protect self-government), but Soldiers in connection with broad exercises of congressional power under the commerce clause (because We the People have spoken). And if judges endorse a moral reading of the Constitution, they might be Heroes with respect to same-sex marriage but Soldiers with respect to economic rights (or vice versa, depending on their preferred moral theory). If judges think that they should infuse the broad language of the Constitution with their own moral judgments, they will be drawn to heroism on important occasions, interpreting the Constitution to protect rights as they understand them.

From these examples, it seems clear that many judges will adopt a Persona in any given case in accordance with their own theory of constitutional interpretation, whether or not that theory is made explicit. In fact, judges may not be self-conscious about their theory; they might not be sure that they have one. (We will turn in later chapters to the idea of "incompletely theorized agreements.") It is also true that many judges lack a simple or unitary theory. They may adopt a Persona on the basis of a collection of considerations that cannot be captured in any kind of theory or "ism." Nonetheless, at least some kind of theory is undoubtedly at work. (See chapter 2 for more details.)

There are some important qualifications. We have seen that judges may adopt a Persona for strategic purposes. They may speak as Minimalists even though their own theory is heroic, and the same is true for second-order Soldiers, who may be Heroes in Soldiers' garb. Judges may act as Mutes, and shut up, even though they would like to be Heroes (and plan to be, when the time is right). I have emphasized that some judges are undoubtedly drawn to a Persona for social or psychological reasons, and as a matter of causation, the Persona might well antedate their adoption of the relevant constitutional theory. Some judges' self-understanding draws them directly to the idea of the Soldier, whereas others are led to minimalism or to enthusiasm for the Hero. Before they even begin to engage with questions of theory, some people greatly admire the idea of heroic judging (as elaborated, for example, by Dworkin or Ely)—whereas to others, that idea seems anathema, lawless, or a form of hubris. In my view, these social or psychological motivations are important and even foundational, but I have acknowledged that this claim remains speculative.

Context

We should also be able to see that different judges may well adopt different Personae in different situations, perhaps because of their preferred approach to constitutional interpretation, perhaps because of contextual considerations. Judges need not be inconsistent or flighty if they are Heroes on one day and Mutes on the next. The difference may be mandated by their preferred approach. Whatever their approach, most judges are likely to believe that there is at least some place for "the passive virtues." When the nation is sharply divided, they might therefore choose to be a Minimalist or a Mute even if they would choose to be a Hero if a national consensus authorized it.

For example, someone who believes in moral readings (as did Bickel, emphatically) might also believe in prudence, and for that reason might believe that silence is golden if courts seek to preserve their own political capital. In the disparaging words of his severe critic, Stanford law professor Gerald Gunther, Bickel thought that courts should be "100 percent principled, 20 percent of the time."[9] Gunther meant this description as an attack on Bickel, but a believer in the passive virtues could easily embrace the characterization without the slightest embarrassment. A judge who believes, with Ely and Justice Breyer, that courts should safeguard and reinforce democratic self-government could similarly agree that there is a time and a place for muteness.

PERSONAE AND IDEOLOGY

Commentators often divide judges along political lines, and reasonably so. A great deal of empirical work shows that in ideologically contested cases, Republican appointees really do vote differently from Democratic appointees. Some judges vote in identifiably conservative directions, and some judges are unmistakable liberals. Of course judicial judgments cannot be reduced to political ones. The law imposes significant constraints, and where it does, it does not matter whether a judge prefers Republicans or Democrats. Nonetheless, political commitments can matter to legal decisions, certainly when the existing legal materials leave gaps or ambiguities. (In chapter 2, we shall explore this point in more detail.)

But we should now be able to see that a central division, not involving ideology as such, is among Personae. As noted, Justice Kennedy is often a Hero, while Chief Justice Roberts is often a Minimalist, while Justice Antonin Scalia is frequently a Hero-Soldier. Consider, for example, Justice Scalia's opinion for the Court in *Heller*, invoking the original understanding in support of the view that the Second Amendment creates an individual right. That opinion was heroic in the important sense that it struck down legislation (though it also had a minimalist dimension insofar as it was relatively narrow). What makes the opinion distinctive is that its heroic and soldierly qualities march hand in hand. Purporting to follow the original understanding—and perhaps actually doing so—Justice Scalia's protection of gun rights was heroic because (in his view) the original understanding so required.

During and after the *Lochner* era, the great liberal judges were Soldiers, voting to uphold progressive legislation that faced serious constitutional challenges. They rejected the heroism of judicial decisions invalidating minimum wage and maximum hour legislation. Celebrated Soldiers (above all Justice Holmes) argued in favor of judicial deference to legislation. During the Warren Court, by contrast, conservatives assumed the mantle of the Soldier. They treated the heroic Warren Court decisions of the 1950s and 1960s as a form of arrogance, hubris, and lawlessness. And indeed, a judge can be heroic on a Tuesday (for example, by voting to invalidate a provision of the Voting Rights Act) and a Soldier on Wednesday (for example, by voting to uphold the Defense of Marriage Act). The rapid switch from Hero to Soldier might seem to be a form of inconsistency, even hypocrisy, but the appearance may well be misleading, for it need not be anything of the kind. The shift might be an artifact of the judge's theory of interpretation.

To qualify as such, all Minimalists are conservative in the sense that they seek to build incrementally on the past. But some Minimalists (as I am understanding them) build incrementally in a liberal direction, whereas others build incrementally to the right. Byron White was a (mostly) liberal Minimalist, as is Ruth Bader Ginsburg, while Chief Justice Roberts is a (mostly) conservative one, as was Sandra Day O'Connor.

There are multiple theories of constitutional muteness, and they need have no political leaning or valence. Both conservatives and liberals can favor muteness. If they are strategic, conservative judges might be silent because they have a long-term plan, which they do not want to compromise by acting prematurely, and liberal judges might behave the same way. As we have seen, some judges embrace an account of Article III, grounded in text and history, that forbids courts from issuing advisory opinions or hearing generalized grievances. That account would produce a number of mute decisions. But we have also seen that by emphasizing "the passive virtues," Bickel meant to draw attention to, and to embrace, quite pragmatic uses of silence, designed to limit the occasions for judicial intervention into the political domain. Bickel did not contend that his own account was required by the text of Article III; his emphasis was on the importance of prudence. And if judges favor self-silencing because they are humble—because they are not too sure that they are right—then humble conservatives and humble liberals might well be able to find common (quiet) ground.

On one view, muteness is an extreme point on the same continuum with minimalism, reflecting a form of judicial statesmanship, and Mutes are Minimalists with less courage (or more prudence). What is clear is that the passive virtues can be enlisted in the service of either conservative or progressive goals.

THE PLOT OF THE PLAY

Which Persona is best? Is it possible to offer criteria by which to answer that question?

I will devote a great deal of attention to these questions in the following chapters. For now, recall that the answer lies in the identification of the right theory of constitutional interpretation. If originalism is the right theory, the appropriate Persona will be an artifact of that theory. So too with judges who embrace a democracy-reinforcing approach to judicial review, or who insist on a moral reading of the founding document. The correct theory is logically prior to the choice among the Constitutional Personae, who may well appear as they do because of the theory that lies in the background.

This is particularly easy to see for Heroes and Soldiers; both of these Personae will fall out of the prevailing theory of interpretation. If you believe in following the original meaning of the Constitution, you might turn out to be a Hero insofar as you vote to protect people's property rights when the government physically invades their land—but you might turn out to be a Soldier when the government regulates commercial advertising. If you believe that courts should protect politically weak groups, you might turn out to be a Hero insofar as you vote to strike down discrimination against the mentally handicapped—but you might turn out to be a Soldier when government adopts affirmative action policies. Recall that which Persona emerges from any particular theory will depend on the constitutional question that is involved.

If an originalist believes in the claims of precedent, he might sound like a Minimalist, because he will want to preserve previous decisions even if he does not agree with them. To the extent that he is willing to abandon the original understanding to protect precedent, he might even turn out to *be* a Minimalist, at least in particular cases. We have seen that muteness may be a product of originalism, but it might also be part of any account of interpretation that insists on an honored place for silence.

No judgment about the role of the courts, or about Constitutional Personae, can sensibly be made in the abstract, or independently of concrete judgments about what can be counted as a mistake, and about who is likely to be trustworthy. In some imaginable worlds, Heroes are heroes; in others, they are hardly that, and they might even be villains. In some imaginable worlds, Soldiers respect democracy without jeopardizing anything of importance; in others, they leave fundamental rights vulnerable to unreliable majorities. In some imaginable worlds, Minimalists strike the proper balance between self-government and other values; in others, they are far too cautious, and their incrementalism is a vice. In some imaginable worlds, Mutes make silence golden; in others, they capitulate to the worst forms of injustice and overreaching.

In short, the right Persona depends on the plot of the play. But to justify that claim, we have to explore the idea of interpretation.

CHAPTER TWO

Interpretation

THE THESIS

Many people believe that the Constitution must be interpreted in their preferred way. They insist that the very idea of interpretation requires judges to adopt their own method of construing the founding document. However abstract and academic-sounding, that is an exceedingly important claim. It suggests that judges are *required* to adopt a particular approach to the Constitution—and that in individual cases, a particular Persona will be a necessary consequence. We have already seen that it is not possible to evaluate a Persona without having a sense of the right theory of interpretation.

The problem is that in the legal context, there is nothing that interpretation "just is." Among the reasonable alternatives, no approach to constitutional interpretation is mandatory. The idea of interpretation is a broad concept, and it can be understood in many different ways. We should see that idea as a kind of umbrella, covering many particular conceptions of what interpretation is. Any particular conception has to be defended, on the merits, as the best one; it cannot be adopted on the ground that it is entailed by the broad concept of interpretation.

I am urging, in short, that whatever their preferred Persona, and whatever their preferred approach, both judges and lawyers must rely on judgments of their own. To some people, that point might seem obvious and trivial. But it is not, because many people, including many judges, seem to think that their own approach is necessary, in the sense that they have no choice but to adopt it, if they are to engage in interpretation at all. That claim is a recipe for confusion. If we abandon that confusion, we will see that adoption of a theory of interpretation is inescapably ours. We cannot avoid making that fundamental choice.

To be sure, we can make a choice that, once made, reduces the authority of the judges—perhaps committing them to be Soldiers, at least most of the time. In fact, some people explicitly argue in favor of making that commitment, and some originalists, including Justices Scalia and Thomas, can be understood as trying to do something like that. What I want to argue here is that their approach must depend on arguments of their own, not on a claim that their approach uniquely fits with the idea of interpretation.

To be sure, some practices cannot count as interpretation at all. If judges do not show fidelity to authoritative texts, they cannot claim to be interpreting them. But without transgressing the legitimate boundaries of interpretation, judges can show fidelity to texts in a variety of ways. Within those boundaries, the choice of approach, among the reasonable alternatives, must depend *on the claim that it makes our constitutional system better rather than worse.* Importantly, this conclusion does not tell us that we should be Heroes, Soldiers, Minimalists, or Mutes. But it does establish the terrain on which the debates must be undertaken.

ON THE VERY IDEA OF INTERPRETATION

Original Intentions

Let's start a bit afield from constitutional law and consider a view about interpretation in general: In interpreting the meaning of words, we ask about the intentions of the author. (I use the term "author" to include speakers as well as writers.) That is just what it means to interpret words.

It is true that in ordinary life, we tend to interpret words in this way. If a friend asks you to meet her at "my favorite restaurant," you will probably ask what, exactly, she had in mind. You will not ask which restaurant you like best, or which restaurant is preferred by your favorite restaurant critic. Ordinary usage might even suggest that in the usual conversational setting, interpretation of people's words amounts to an effort to elicit their intentions. Of course, this conclusion invites attention to context and purposes, not just the literal meaning of people's words. If a friend tells you, "bring me the cell," you will not look up the word "cell" in the dictionary and choose the first definition; you probably know that she means "cell phone." And if a friend makes some kind of linguistic error, you would not want to hold her to those words. But if you depart from her words, it is because you are trying to figure out what she had in mind.

Some people think that legal interpretation is not fundamentally different. In their view, a form of originalism, based on the idea of authorial intention, is built into the concept of interpretation. For example, University of San Diego law professor Larry Alexander writes that "given what we accept as legally authoritative, the proper way to interpret the Constitution ... is to seek its authors' intended meanings—the same thing we do when we read a letter from Mom, a shopping list from our spouse, or instructions for how to assemble a child's toy made in China."[1] Walter Benn Michaels, a distinguished professor of literature, goes even further: "In fact, however, you can't do textual interpretation without some appeal to authorial intention and, perhaps more controversially, you can't (coherently and nonarbitrarily) think of yourself as still doing textual interpretation as soon as you appeal to something beyond authorial intention—for example, the original public meaning or evolving principles of justice."[2]

Note that Alexander and Michaels are making some very strong claims. Alexander contends that interpretation of the Constitution is best understood, or perhaps just is, a search for the authors' intended meanings. Michaels thinks that if you do not try to find out what the author intended, you are not engaged in interpretation at all. On this view, the choice of Persona is easy: You look for the intended meaning, and you have the Persona that follows. (Sure, it can be challenging to discover the intended meaning, especially if we are speaking of the intentions of numerous people centuries ago—but I want to bracket that point for now.)

It is true that if we wanted, we could define legal interpretation in this way. But do we really have to? Not at all. On that count, Alexander and Michaels are wrong.

Let's back up a bit and suppose that in ordinary conversation, most people understand the idea of interpretation to involve a search for authorial intentions. Even in ordinary conversation, such an understanding is not really mandatory. We could at least imagine the view that interpretation involves a search for public meaning—for the ordinary meaning of the words in the English language—rather than authorial intentions. But we should not be too fussy here. It is certainly sensible to say that in conversation, we usually ask about intentions. If this is indeed sensible, it is for a pragmatic reason; the goal of the particular communication will be defeated if we do not.

When a friend asks me to meet her or to do something for her, I am likely to ask about her intentions, because I want to meet her or do what she wants. It is for this reason that if my friend says that we should "meet at the best restaurant in town," I will likely ask what she meant by those words. It is imaginable, of course, that she wants me to do a little work and to see what the restaurant critics like best—but if so, I am still trying to follow her subjective intentions. If interpretation entails a search for intentions, the reason is that in the relevant context, that is the best way to understand the term, because that makes the interaction work in the best way that it can.

The same things might be said about communication in workplaces with an established hierarchy. Suppose that your supervisor tells you to do something. If so, it is right to think that in ordinary circumstances, you ought to ask: "What, exactly, did my supervisor intend to mean by that?" (The qualification "in ordinary circumstances" is necessary because even if you have a supervisor, you will sometimes ask about something other than his intentions; everything depends on your role. You might be allowed to ask yourself whether you are able to achieve the supervisor's goal in a way that is different from the specific instruction; perhaps the supervisor's general purpose, and not his intention, is what most matters.) You ask this question, if you do, for pragmatic reasons. Employees should generally follow the instructions of their supervisors; that is usually what it means to be an employee. The practice of following instructions, in hierarchical organizations, generally requires close attention to supervisors' subjective intentions.

For these reasons, it is plausible to say that in some contexts, interpretation of the instructions of a supervisor "just is" an effort to elicit and follow the supervisor's intentions. This is so not in the sense that this understanding of interpretation is literally inevitable or strictly mandatory or is built into the very idea of interpretation. But it is so in the important sense that it captures how most people use the term "interpretation" in such contexts. If that is true, it is because this understanding of interpretation makes the supervisor-employee relationship work best. If you don't follow the supervisor's intention, that relationship will be damaged.

True, some people think that constitutional interpretation is just like that. Good Soldiers believe that they are in a sense employees, and We the People are their supervisors. As Soldiers, judges have to ask what their supervisors meant. And that is a possible view. The problem lies in the words "have to." A judge need not treat the authors of the Constitution the same way that an employee treats the words of a supervisor. We will get to that point in due course. For the moment, let's simply notice that employees do, in fact, care a lot about their supervisors' intentions.

Some people believe that in many contexts, it is not even possible to interpret people's words without making some kind of judgment about the author's intentions. On this view, the idea of meaning depends on some such judgment, and it is incoherent without it. Outside of law, the claim is disputed; perhaps the conventions of language can enable us to know what words mean, without resorting to intentions. (If someone says, "saddle up that horse," or "be sure to meet me at 9 a.m." we know what that person means, and we don't have to worry over his intentions.) But in the legal context, the claim that meaning depends on people's intentions is plainly false, as we shall now see.

Original Meaning

One conception of interpretation involves a search for a speaker's intention, and in ordinary life, that is the most common conception. But it is easy to think of cases, certainly in law, in which interpretation does not operate by reference to such intentions. Many Heroes do not consult the intentions of those who wrote or ratified the Constitution, and the same is true of many Soldiers.

In fact, some of the most committed originalists, including Justice Scalia himself, believe that what matters is the *original public meaning* of the document, not intentions at all.[3] There is a real difference between the two approaches. The original public meaning can be ascertained without investigating anyone's subjective intentions. And while the two will often produce the same answer, they might diverge. In his heroic opinion in *Heller*, for example, Justice Scalia wrote that in "interpreting [the Second Amendment], we are guided by the principle that '[t]he Constitution was written to be understood by the voters; its words and phrases were used in their normal and ordinary as distinguished from technical meaning.'" In his view, "Normal meaning may of course include an idiomatic meaning, but it excludes secret or technical meanings that would not have been known to ordinary citizens in the founding generation."[4]

Originalists themselves argue fiercely about whether the original meaning, or instead the original intentions, should be taken as authoritative—a point that suggests that interpretation, to qualify as such, need not be focused on intentions. This might seem to be a technical distinction, but recall that our general question is whether the idea of interpretation requires any particular approach. The fact that many people focus on original meaning is a strong point against those who argue, with Alexander and Michaels, that interpretation is just a search for the author's intentions. Those who focus on original public meaning argue that meaning is objective, not subjective. In their view, what matters is the standard understanding among the Constitution's ratifiers, not what the authors "intended." After all, the ratifiers (We the People), and not the authors, turned the Constitution into law. Rejecting subjective intentions, Justice Holmes wrote, "We do not inquire what the legislature meant; we ask only what the statutes mean."[5]

Of course those who insist on adherence to the original public meaning count as originalists—but they do not rely on subjective intentions. At this point, my goal is not to take a stand on originalism, or on which form of originalism is best or most coherent, or to suggest that the original meaning must be taken as fixed and binding. (The very idea of original meaning has more than one meaning.) It is only to insist that a prominent understanding of originalism—as involving public meaning rather than intentions—is enough to demonstrate that attention to subjective intentions is not built into the very idea of interpretation.

CONSEQUENCES

Is it plausible to say that interpretation *necessarily* entails a search for the original public meaning? Not at all. I have not endorsed Alexander's claims in any way, but he is plainly right to suggest that interpretation often does involve an inquiry into intentions rather than public meaning. (Recall that if your friend says, "let's go to the best movie now playing," you will probably ask what she has in mind, not what is generally recognized as best, unless that is what she has in mind.) We could also imagine a form of textualism, and hence an approach to interpretation, that inquires about *contemporary* meaning—thus calling for adherence to the current, rather than the historical, meaning of the constitutional text. Both Heroes and Minimalists sometimes seem to favor this approach. They ask whether a law—say, one that discriminates on the basis of sex—is consistent with the requirement of "equal protection of the laws" in the contemporary sense, and the same is true when people object that restrictions on campaign contributions violate "the freedom of speech." To their credit, many of those who insist on fidelity to the original meaning candidly acknowledge that their own view is not compelled by the very idea of interpretation. Instead they suggest that their own approach would lead to better consequences.

For example, Justice Scalia stresses the risks associated with judicial discretion, and he contends that if judges adhere to original meaning, those risks will be diminished, because unelected judges will be constrained. Some originalists focus on the goal of democratic self-government, and they argue that if judges respect the original meaning, they will promote that goal. Consider the illuminating suggestion by Randy Barnett: "Given a sufficiently good constitutional text, originalists maintain that better results will be reached overall if government officials—including judges—must stick to the original meaning rather than empowering them to trump that meaning with one that they prefer."[6] This is a candid argument that the case for originalism depends on what will produce "better results" overall. If Heroes and Soldiers emerge from the approach that does in fact produce better results, all should be well.

Of special importance here is Barnett's emphasis on the need for a "sufficiently good constitutional text," understood in light of the original meaning. That is an important acknowledgment. Suppose that the constitutional text, taken only as such and without reference to original meaning, is good, or good enough. But suppose that from the standpoint of democratic self-government and human rights, it is a *great deal worse if it is understood in light of its original meaning*. Imagine, for example, that it is hopelessly undemocratic, or that it entrenches racial injustice. If so, the argument for sticking with the original meaning would be severely weakened.

In fact, this is not an implausible account of the American Constitution. The text itself contains broadly appealing phrases, protecting "the freedom of speech" and guaranteeing "due process of law" and "the equal protection of the laws" and vesting executive power in "a president of the United States." There is a good argument that if these words were construed in accordance with their original meaning—at least if that meaning is understood in terms of the originally expected applications[7]—our constitutional order would be far worse than it is today.

For example, we would surely have to authorize racial segregation by the national government and probably the states as well. Almost certainly, sex discrimination would be acceptable. Our free speech principle would be sharply truncated. The basic point is that if we really stuck with the original meaning, our constitutional system would not deserve quite the celebration that it now rightly receives.

Heroes, Soldiers, and Minimalists have played a large role in interpreting the text so as to produce that admirable system—and their
interpretations have not followed either the original intention or the
original meaning. (Mutes have played only a bit part.)

True, we should enthusiastically agree that judges ought to be faithful
to the text itself, even if the text were not as good as it is. Interpretation
entails fidelity. If judges were not faithful to the text, it is fair to say that
they would not be engaged in interpretation at all. If judges disregard
authoritative texts, including the Constitution, they cannot claim to be
interpreting them. In that sense, the idea of interpretation does impose
constraints on what judges may do. There is nothing that interpretation
just is, but there are some things that interpretation just isn't.

Moreover, legal systems do much better—and even count as legal
systems—if the judges who operate within them are faithful to authoritative texts. If they do not, the rule of law is itself in jeopardy, because
judges would appear to be empowered to do whatever they want. They
could go off on larks on their own, reducing predictability and increasing the risk of arbitrary exercises of discretion. In that sense, there are
excellent arguments, rooted in the rule of law, in favor of taking constitutional texts as binding. But under the assumptions I have given, why
should judges stick not merely with the text but also with its original
meaning? If the consequences of sticking with it would be terrible,
and if those consequences could be avoided with another approach,
shouldn't judges consider that other approach?

These questions are not meant to be rhetorical; they suggest only
that various approaches to interpretation—different conceptions of that
broad concept—are legitimately on the table. Many originalists find it
both appropriate and necessary to argue that the consequences of their
approach would not be terrible. With Barnett, they urge that those
consequences would be good. They contend that their approach fits
with a great deal of existing judicial doctrine, or at least with those
aspects of it—whether heroic or soldierly—that seem least dispensable.

For example, few contemporary originalists are willing to concede that under their approach, racial segregation is constitutionally acceptable—even though nothing in the original meaning bans segregation by the national government, and even though it is not at all easy to show that the Constitution bans segregation at the state level. Few contemporary originalists agree that their approach would allow the national government to prohibit women from working for the federal civil service or would freely allow states to discriminate against women.

On the contrary, originalists tend either to say little about the difficulty in squaring their approach with many of the most basic commitments of the contemporary constitutional order or to insist that the difficulty is not so severe, because originalism already embodies those commitments. Some originalists work extremely hard to try to demonstrate that point and to show that the great achievement of past interpretive Heroes, Soldiers, and Minimalists can be maintained. They are right to do so, because the argument for their approach is greatly weakened without that work. (Would we really want to endorse an approach to interpretation that deemed the great achievements of the past to be illegitimate?) Whether or not that argument is convincing, what is noteworthy is that many of those who stress original meaning find it necessary to stress these points about consequences. (Recall that they do not rest content with, or even make, the claim that their approach is built into the very idea of interpretation.)

Indeed, some originalists, notably Jack Balkin, insist that certain provisions of the Constitution are written in general and abstract terms, which allow accommodation of evolving understandings.[8] On Balkin's view, originalism requires respect for the original "semantic meaning," which does not require fidelity to expected applications, and which includes broad terms that are subject to "construction," in a way that invites change, even heroism. Balkin thinks, for example, that the reach of the equal protection clause is not settled by the original understanding of whether that clause would forbid discrimination on the basis of sex or sexual orientation. Judges must follow the words, but not necessarily the original understanding of how they should be specifically applied. (I will turn to the distinction between interpretation and construction in due course.) That position certainly leaves a lot of room for heroism.

Some people who hold this view contend that the original understanding was that the Constitution creates broad principles whose concrete meaning would not be frozen in time.[9] Suppose that their claim is historical—that it is about the intended meaning, or about the public meaning, at the time. If it is taken as a claim about the views of Americans in the late eighteenth century, it is not clear that it is right; the historical evidence is ambiguous here, and those who have consulted the historical record are divided on what approach to interpretation was sought by those who wrote and ratified the founding document. (There may be no purely historical answer to that question. As Gertrude Stein once said of Oakland, "There is no there there.") But if the original understanding did in fact contemplate interpretive change over time, the line between originalism and other approaches starts to dissolve, because interpretation of abstractions—what counts as "equal protection" or "the freedom of speech"—squarely invites the exercise of discretion on the part of the judges. And if Balkin's approach to interpretation is correct, my main conclusion holds: It is not because of anything intrinsic to the idea of interpretation, but because its adoption would make our constitutional system better rather than worse. And if so, judges get to be Heroes or Soldiers not because the original understanding mandates that role, but because in some sense, that is what they want to be.

FIT AND JUSTIFICATION

I have emphasized that the concept of interpretation does impose constraints. Some approaches cannot qualify as interpretation at all. Even if it would be good, pragmatically speaking, to substitute the best imaginable constitution for our own constitution, the substitution cannot count as interpretation. But the concept of interpretation does not compel any form of originalism. Let us now turn to other approaches. Suppose a judge thinks that where the Constitution is vague or open-textured, he should interpret it to make the democratic process work as well as it possibly can—an idea that (as we have seen) John Hart Ely and Justice Breyer have vigorously championed. Is that approach ruled off-limits by the very idea of interpretation? It is hard to see why. Justice Breyer has argued that a democracy-protecting approach, honoring what he calls "active liberty" (referring to public participation in governance) fits with the text and purposes of the document even if it does not fit with the original meaning, narrowly conceived. (Recall that some originalists think that the Constitution was deliberately written in broad terms whose meaning was meant to evolve over time.) As an approach to interpretation, Breyer's approach is certainly a candidate, and it must be evaluated on its merits; it cannot be ruled off the table. To his credit, Breyer is candid about this point and contends that the consequences of his preferred approach would be good—and that any approach to interpretation must stand or fall on its consequences.

Something similar can be said about Ronald Dworkin's preferred view, which (it will be recalled) is that the Constitution should be taken to include abstractions that invite self-conscious and explicitly moral reasoning from judges, and that judges must give those generalities the best moral readings that they can.[10] That approach certainly invites a degree of heroism. On Dworkin's view, judges try to understand terms like "the freedom of speech" and "equal protection of the laws" in ways that make moral sense. Indeed, both the *Lochner* Court and the Warren Court approached the Constitution in this way, and many admirers of Heroes, on both the right and the left, think the Court should resume something like this approach today. Whether or not it is the right approach, it would certainly count as interpretation within permissible linguistic understandings of the term.

Dworkin has argued that legal interpretation involves two obligations.[11] The first obligation is one of "fit"; an interpreter cannot simply ignore the materials that are being interpreted. The second is one of "justification." What Dworkin means is that within the constraints of fit, an interpreter must justify the existing legal materials in the sense of making them the best that they can be. To explain this approach, Dworkin offers the arresting analogy of a chain novel. Suppose that you are the fifth writer in a chain, and that your task is to write the novel's fifth chapter. Four writers have written four chapters before you. In writing the fifth chapter, you must write the novel that others have started, and not another. You cannot make up a whole new novel. Nor can you depart from what has come before, in the sense of producing a narrative that ignores it or makes it unintelligible or random. But you might well think that you have an obligation to make the novel good rather than terrible, and your authorship of the next chapter will be undertaken with that obligation in mind.

Dworkin is right to observe that at least in a system that is based on precedent, judicial judgments often seem a lot like that, as Heroes, Soldiers, Minimalists, and Mutes should all acknowledge. It is generally agreed that in the American constitutional system, judges who interpret the Constitution owe a duty of fidelity to the decisions that have come before (acknowledging that if past decisions are clearly wrong, they might be overruled). But in dealing with those decisions, judges also have a degree of discretion. They can turn the tale in one direction or another. If, for example, the question is whether the Constitution requires states to recognize same-sex marriage, they must ask, What approach makes the best sense out of the existing materials?

They might think that in light of decisions barring states from forbidding racial intermarriage, and invalidating criminal bans on same-sex sodomy, the best way to continue the tale is to say that states may not forbid two adults from marrying, even if they are both men or both women. That would be a heroic decision and in 2015, the Court chose heroism. Or they might think that even in light of those decisions, the best way to continue the tale is to say that because states have traditionally been able to define marriage as they wish (so long as racial discrimination is involved), it is lawful to ban same-sex marriage. That would be a soldierly decision. In either case, judges are engaged in interpretation in the sense that they are trying to remain faithful to what has come before ("fit") while also making the existing materials as sensible and appealing as possible ("justification").

Of course it is true that an emphasis on fit and justification leaves many questions open. A recurring question is the relationship among past judicial decisions, society's past practices, and the original understanding of the text; what does the obligation of fit mean when these point in different directions? Different answers to that question are admissible within the general concept of interpretation. Democracy-reinforcement (as defended by Ely and Breyer) is one attempt at an answer; so is originalism, focused as it is on the authoritative text and original understandings (with some originalists, such as Justice Scalia, emphasizing that precedent can have priority over the original understanding, and other originalists, such as Justice Thomas, insisting that the original understanding generally has priority).

On the basis of Dworkin's argument, we might be tempted to think (as Dworkin does) that there is one thing that legal interpretation just is: an attempt to ensure both fit and justification. And it is true that Heroes, Soldiers, Minimalists, and Mutes can accept the view that both fit and justification matter. But that temptation should be resisted. While Dworkin's approach is one conception of interpretation, it is not the only one. If we believe, with Alexander and Michaels, that interpretation involves the search for authorial intentions, we will not much care about justification. We will attempt to identify a fact: What did the author(s) intend? It is true that the answer to that question might be difficult to find, and it is also true that there may be no answer to that question. But if so, we may have exhausted the act of interpretation. (Something similar can be said about those who emphasize the original public meaning.) At least that is one view (again, not the only one) of what interpretation is.

INTERPRETATION AND CONSTRUCTION

With a point of this kind in mind, some people have insisted on the great importance of making a distinction between "interpretation" and "construction."[12] In an especially clear and illuminating discussion, Georgetown University legal theorist Lawrence Solum suggests that interpretation attempts to discover the linguistic or semantic meaning of a legal text, whereas construction gives legal effect to that meaning.[13] The First Amendment, for example, has a linguistic meaning ("no law abridging"), and no one can argue that the linguistic meaning, by itself, is identical to particular First Amendment doctrines: the lower level of protection accorded to commercial advertising, the exclusion of bribery, the distinction between content-based restrictions on speech ("no one may criticize the President") and content-neutral restrictions ("no one may march in high-traffic streets during working hours").

Solum urges that interpretation, taken as such, "is guided by linguistic facts—facts about patterns of usage"[14] and is in that respect value-free or only "thinly normative," in the sense that our own evaluations about what the law should be are not relevant to the question whether an interpretation is correct. By contrast, "theories of construction are ultimately normative," in the sense that a judgment on behalf of one construction rather than another turns on "premises that go beyond linguistic facts." In Solum's terminology, an approach that favors deference to the political process, and hence soldiering, is a theory of construction. It does not come from the linguistic meaning of anything in the Constitution itself, and to defend it, judges have to offer evaluations of their own. But when judges decide to be Soldiers, they do not enlist their own moral or political beliefs in particular cases. In fact, that is one of the goals of soldiering—to rule those beliefs entirely off-limits. We have seen that Justice Holmes, the iconic Soldier, sought to do exactly that.

When the linguistic meaning of a text is vague (as it seems to be for many constitutional provisions), then the fact that judges are involved in construction, rather than interpretation (in the sense of uncovering linguistic meaning), seems obvious. On Solum's view, interpretation gives rise to a "construction zone." For judges who find themselves in that zone, there are many ways to proceed; soldiering, or deference to the political process, is merely one. Heroes of course choose another.

If we accept this distinction, then we might say that there is nothing that *construction* just is, because construction cannot occur without some kind of justification for proceeding one way rather than another, and because several (or many) plausible justifications are consistent with the basic idea of construction. When Soldiers and Heroes disagree, it is because they have radically different views about the best kind of construction—and they should be aware that those views are their own. But on this view, there is something that *interpretation* just is, which is the elicitation of linguistic meaning. For this reason, some version of textualism—in Solum's own account, one that is rooted in the original public meaning—is a necessary foundation for interpretation. The word "speech," for example, cannot mean "Mars," or "president," or "horse," or "flood," or "ketchup," and the words "due process" cannot mean "with pan-cakes," or "American slavery," or "long-burning candle." In the eighteenth century, the word "goal" (often spelled "gaol") meant "jail," and if we read an eighteenth-century legal text using that word, we might well insist on the original public meaning to interpret it.

But there's a problem with this claim as well. As Solum acknowledges, there are different approaches to the identification of linguistic meaning. Original intention and original meaning are two, and as we have seen, it would also be possible to identify linguistic meaning by pointing to contemporary understandings (as Heroes often do). For words like "freedom of speech" and "equal protection," the very idea of interpretation does not rule out the use of contemporary understandings. It is true that in the case of an eighteenth-century text with the word "goal," we would be drawn to some form of originalism. (The same is true of the words "domestic violence" in the Constitution; it would be pretty ridiculous to understand that term to refer to spousal abuse.) And interpreters do have to attend to linguistic meaning. But there is nothing in the idea of interpretation that resolves disputes between those who favor the original meaning and those who favor the contemporary meaning.

Interpretation, understood as the search for linguistic meaning, is an important and even critical part of the obligation of "fit"—and it is distinctive and perhaps has special (unique) priority, because it fastens on the obligation to attend to the semantic meaning of authoritative texts. All of the Personae might well agree on that proposition. For my purposes here, however, it is necessary to see that more than one approach can plausibly be treated as interpretive, and that in many cases, the idea of construction is doing all the crucial work. Again: Heroes and Soldiers, for example, have legitimate disagreements, and the disagreements involve their competing understandings of the best way to do constitutional law.

DECISION COSTS AND ERROR COSTS

I have suggested that identification of the proper approach to constitutional interpretation requires attention whether it would make our constitutional order better or worse. Here is a way to specify that abstract claim and to make it a bit more tractable: An approach to the Constitution might impose two kinds of costs. It might impose decision costs, by complicating judicial judgments, and it might impose error costs, by producing bad outcomes.

Without making the ludicrous claim that these ideas should be understood in purely economic terms, we can insist that in deciding on their preferred approach to interpretation, judges should consider the decisional burdens imposed by one or another approach to the founding document. If all judges became Soldiers and declared that they would uphold any legislation unless the constitutional violation were clear, they would certainly lower the costs of decisions, simply because almost all legislation would be immediately upheld. For judges, application of a soldierly approach is generally straightforward. Originalists believe that their approach also lowers decision costs, and in particular, that it promotes the rule of law, by increasing clarity and predictability.

For Minimalists, the assessment is more complex. To the extent that Minimalists focus narrowly on particular problems, minimalism imposes modest decisional burdens—at least in specific cases. But because minimalists leave so much undecided, those burdens, or costs, might be faced by judges or by others, including legislators, members of the executive branch, and citizens themselves, who must eventually pay the cost of uncertainty.

But it is also important to consider the number and the magnitude of errors. True, reasonable people disagree about whether certain outcomes count as errors at all. But there would be serious reason to question any approach to the Constitution that would declare race and sex discrimination to be unobjectionable, or that would raise serious constitutional doubts about practices that the president and Congress have accepted for many decades. If an approach would greatly unsettle longstanding institutional practices, there is reason to question it for that reason alone. If an approach would badly compromise democratic self-government, it would be objectionable for that reason (though the intensity of the objection depends on how we specify the nature and limits of that ideal). And if an approach would eliminate or undermine rights that Americans enjoy, and deserve to enjoy, then the approach is questionable on that very ground. Here, too, we can identify the grounds on which Heroes depart from Soldiers. To Heroes, Soldiers leave far too much at risk, including the rights to freedom of speech and free exercise of religion.

Judges might agree that the choice among interpretive approaches depends on what approach makes our constitutional order best, but sharply disagree about which approach does that. In my view, a disagreement of this kind helps to separate people who are committed to different approaches to constitutional interpretation—and helps explain why (for example) few people are consistent Soldiers. Nearly everyone would agree that if an approach is inconsistent with *Brown v. Board of Education* or with *Loving v. Virginia* (striking down bans on racial intermarriage), it runs into problems for that reason. And nearly everyone would agree that if an approach would license judges to invalidate legislation whenever they liked, it would be unacceptable for that reason as well. Any approach has to constrain judicial discretion.

All this should be common ground. But some questions are far more contested. If one or another approach to interpretation would mean that the Constitution protects no right of privacy, does that count against that approach, or in its favor? With respect to privacy, do we want more Heroes or more Soldiers? Or perhaps Minimalists and Mutes? Reasonable people disagree. If an approach would reduce constitutional protection of rights, is that a terrible problem, or might it be not so bad in light of the possibility (likelihood?) that the democratic process would respect and protect such rights on its own? We can easily imagine disagreements about such questions. Notably, they would have a significant empirical dimension. One question is this: If judges receded, what would the democratic process end up doing?

Often there is sufficient agreement to permit diverse people to engage with one another about appropriate approaches. But it must be emphasized that some arguments about the appropriate approach to interpretation are (implicitly) disputes about what kinds of results count as errors.

POSSIBLE WORLDS

We can go further. No approach to constitutional law makes sense in every imaginable nation or in every possible world. The argument for any Persona, and for any particular approach, must depend, in large part, on a set of judgments about institutional capacities—above all, about the strengths and weaknesses of legislatures and courts. We cannot assess decision costs and error costs without making those judgments. If judges are excellent and error-free, their excellence bears on the choice of a theory of interpretation (and argues in favor of more heroism). If judges are likely to blunder, their fallibility bears on the choice of a theory of interpretation (and argues in favor of more soldiering).

Return to the Soldier's view: Courts should uphold legislation unless it is plainly and unambiguously in violation of the Constitution. Few people now accept that position, which finds no support on the contemporary Supreme Court. We have seen that because the Constitution is frequently ambiguous, the Soldier's approach would require courts to uphold almost all legislation—including school segregation in the District of Columbia, sex discrimination in federal employment, affirmative action, restrictions on abortion, deviations from the idea of one person, one vote, mandatory school prayer, and much more. In these circumstances, it should be unsurprising that most judges assert their right to interpret the Constitution independently, refusing to accept the legislature's view merely because the document is ambiguous. In the last half-century, no member of the Court has been willing to embrace across-the-board soldiering and to endorse the proposition that legislation should be upheld unless the founding document is entirely clear.

But in principle, we should not disparage soldiering for that reason. Imagine a society in which democratic processes work exceedingly fairly and well, so that judicial intervention is almost never required from the standpoint of anything that really matters. In such a society, racial segregation does not occur. Political processes are fair, and political speech is never banned. People are treated with dignity. The legitimate claims of religious minorities and property holders are respected. The systems of federalism and separation of powers are safeguarded, and precisely to the right extent, by democratic institutions. Both self-government and human rights are given their proper scope.

Imagine too that in this society, judicial judgments are highly unreliable. From the standpoint of political morality, judges make systematic blunders when they attempt to specify constitutional terms such as "equal protection of the laws" and "due process of law." Resolving constitutional questions without respecting the views of the legislature, courts would make society worse, because their understandings of rights and institutions are so bad. In such a society, the Soldier's approach to the Constitution would make a great deal of sense, and judges should be persuaded to adopt it. These are extreme assumptions, of course, but even if they are softened significantly, the argument for soldiering might be convincing, all things considered.

Many people reject the idea of minimalism. But imagine a society in which the original public meaning of the Constitution, from very long ago, is not so excellent, in the sense that it does not adequately protect rights, properly understood, and in the sense that it calls for institutional arrangements (say, between Congress and the president) that become obsolete over time, as new circumstances and fresh needs arise. Imagine that in this society, the democratic process is good but not great, in the sense that it sometimes produces or permits significant injustices. Suppose finally that in this society, judges will do poorly if they really seek to strike out on their own, or if they attempt to build doctrine on the basis of high-level theory, but very well if they build modestly and incrementally on their own precedents, following something like the common-law method. In such a society, a minimalist approach to the Constitution would have a great deal to commend it. In such a society, maybe most of us would be Minimalists.

Or consider a society in which democratic processes work exceedingly poorly, in the sense that they do not live up to democratic ideals, and also in which political majorities invade fundamental rights—say, freedom of religion and freedom of speech. In that society, human dignity is not respected. Suppose by contrast that in this society, judges are trustworthy, in the sense that they can make democratic processes work much better (say, by safeguarding the right to vote), and also that they can protect fundamental rights, as they really should be understood. In such a society, judges make the right judgments about justice. They are essentially unerring. In such a society, the argument for a form of heroism—democracy-reinforcement and moral readings—would be quite strong.

We should now be able to see that multiple Personae, and a range of approaches to interpretation, are compatible with the Constitution itself. No single Persona, and no single approach, is dictated by the founding document. If that document set out the rules for its own interpretation, judges would be bound by those rules (though any such rules would themselves need to be interpreted). But the Constitution sets out no such rules. It does not say that judges or others, attempting to interpret the document, should be Soldiers, Minimalists, Heroes, or Mutes. For this reason, any approach to the document must be defended by reference to some account that is supplied by the interpreter.

The meaning of the Constitution must be made rather than found, not in the sense that it is entirely up for grabs, but in the sense that it must be settled by an account of interpretation that it does not itself contain. Any particular approach to the Constitution, and the adoption of any Persona, must be defended on the ground that it makes the relevant constitutional order better rather than worse. I now offer a qualified defense of my own preferred Persona, who turns out to be a distinctive kind of Minimalist.

CHAPTER THREE

Burkean Minimalism

WE HAVE SEEN enough to conclude that no Persona makes sense for all times and seasons. In my view, however, the Minimalist has particular appeal, certainly in constitutional law, and if we have to opt for a preferred Persona, we should choose the Minimalist. As I have emphasized, people are often attracted to one or another Persona for psychological and sociological reasons, but in the end, we need to have reasons, not attractions.

The principal goal of this chapter is to offer reasons in support of the Minimalist. The other Personae will make occasional (and significant) appearances, but largely by way of contrast. I focus on minimalism in part because it is (in my view) far more attractive than it might seem at first glance, and in part because it has an enduring and insufficiently appreciated role in American constitutional law (as well as the constitutional law of many other legal systems). At the same time, there are reasonable objections to minimalism, and, in the process of the discussion, we shall see what the Hero and the Soldier have to say by way of response. (The Mute will get in a few words as well.)

I also aim to show that there are two principal siblings in the minimalist family: Burkeans, who give a great deal of weight to traditions, and rationalists, who also favor small steps, but who require traditions to have some kind of justification. Within the family, the siblings have strong disagreements. I will also identify the circumstances in which one or another form of minimalism makes the most sense. As we shall see, Burkean minimalism has especially strong claims in the area of separation of powers, where traditions should be given careful consideration. But the rationalist alternative has especially strong claims under the equal protection clause, where it is appropriate for judges to question traditions, rather than to accept them.

To orient the discussion, consider the following cases:

1. For more than fifty years, the words "under God" have been part of the Pledge of Allegiance. Some parents object to the use of those words in schools where it is mandatory to say the pledge, arguing that under current constitutional principles, the reference to God must be counted as an establishment of religion, forbidden by the First Amendment.

2. For more than seventy years, the Supreme Court has permitted Congress to create "independent" regulatory agencies—agencies whose heads are immune from the unlimited removal power of the president. Independent agencies include the Federal Reserve Board, the Federal Communications Commission, and the Federal Trade Commission. The Department of Justice now attacks the whole notion of "independence," arguing that it is inconsistent with the system of checks and balances under any reasonable understanding of that system. The Department of Justice asks the Supreme Court to rule that the idea of independence is unconstitutional—and that the president must be able to control all those who execute national law.

3. The president of the United States has long engaged in "foreign surveillance" by wiretapping conversations in which at least one of the

parties is in another nation and is suspected of being unfriendly to the United States. The practice of foreign surveillance has been upheld by several lower courts, which see that practice as falling within the president's "inherent" authority. Those subject to such surveillance argue that as originally understood, the Constitution cannot be construed to grant such "inherent" authority to the president. They want the federal courts to rule that the president lacks that authority.

4. For many decades, presidents have made recess appointments when a vacancy "exists" during the recess, even if the vacancy did not "arise" during the recess. There is a strong argument, based on the text of the Constitution and its original meaning, that this practice is unconstitutional. Those who accept this argument add that presidential practices cannot overcome the natural meaning of the Constitution itself. In court, people contend that an agency cannot act if it is led by people who have been appointed through an unlawful recess appointment—and they ask the Supreme Court to rule accordingly.

Each of these cases presents a conflict between longstanding practices and what is plausibly argued to be the best interpretation of the original Constitution. Those who challenge the practices contend that the best interpretation must prevail. They argue on behalf of heroism. A predictable response is that when construing the Constitution, courts should be closely attentive to entrenched practices and must give deference to the judgments of public officials extending over time. On this view, constitutional interpretation should be conservative in the literal sense—respecting settled judicial doctrine, but also deferring to traditions as such.

Sometimes those who make such arguments embrace soldiering; they want the courts to uphold longstanding practices. But often they adopt an approach to constitutional law that I shall call *Burkean minimalism*. Followers of Edmund Burke are Minimalists by nature, and those who adopt the Minimalist Persona might consider the term a redundancy. But as we are about to see, some Minimalists are not Burkeans, and hence it is not redundant to identify Burkean minimalism as such. Burkean minimalism is my principal topic here, in part because it offers an attractive approach to constitutional law, and in part because a focus on Burkean Minimalists is an especially helpful way to see what might be said for and against the various Personae.

Burkean Minimalists believe that constitutional principles must be built incrementally and by analogy, and with close reference to longstanding practices. All Minimalists insist on incrementalism; but committed Burkeans also emphasize the need for judges to pay careful attention to established traditions and to avoid or cabin independent moral and political argument of any kind.

On this count, Burkean Minimalists disagree sharply with Heroes. But they should also be distinguished from their more rationalistic counterparts, who are less focused on longstanding practices, and who are far more willing to require an independent justification for those practices. Rationalist minimalists insist on reasons, and as a result, they are a distinctive breed. For example, they might well attack discrimination on the basis of sex and sexual orientation. Because they require independent justifications, they may well make common cause with Heroes, and Burkeans greatly distrust them for that reason.

In the nation's history, Justices Felix Frankfurter and Sandra Day O'Connor have been the most prominent practitioners of Burkean minimalism, in the sense that they have tended to favor small steps and close attention to both experience and tradition. In major separation of powers cases, Chief Justice William Rehnquist and Justice Stephen Breyer have also shown keen interest in Burkean minimalism.

One of my goals in this chapter is to identify the ingredients of Burkean minimalism—an approach that has both integrity and coherence, that has played a large role in the history of American constitutional thought, and that casts fresh light on a number of contemporary disputes. I also aim to answer a simple question: Under what assumptions and conditions would Burkean minimalism be most appealing? An anti-Burkean approach, subjecting traditions to critical scrutiny, has played a large role in the domains of race and sex discrimination; in these areas, and others that involve equality, there is a strong argument for rationalist Minimalists and even for Heroes. In areas in which traditions are unjust and in which judges can reliably assess them in constitutionally relevant terms, we should reject Burkean minimalism. Bans on same-sex marriage as an example.

The case for Burkean minimalism is most plausible when three conditions are met: (1) originalism would produce unacceptable consequences, (2) longstanding traditions and practices are trustworthy or at least trustworthy enough, and (3) there is great reason to be skeptical of the rule-elaborating and theory-building capacities of federal judges. Those who tend to accept Burkean minimalism—above all Justices Frankfurter and O'Connor—apparently believe that these three conditions are pervasive.

As we shall see, the argument for Burkean minimalism is extremely strong in the areas of separation of powers and national security, where the Court rightly gives attention to longstanding practices. As we shall also see, Burkean minimalism bears on a number of unresolved and increasingly pressing dilemmas in contemporary constitutional law, ranging from the protection of individual rights to the question of presidential authority to the appropriately minimalist response to heroic precedents.

CONSERVATIVE CONSTITUTIONAL THEORY

Within conservative constitutional thought, Burkean minimalism is both popular and time-honored. But it is opposed by those who adopt two alternative approaches. We have seen the first: originalism. It is noteworthy that the great conservative dissenters on the Warren Court,

Justices Frankfurter and John Marshall Harlan, had strong minimalist inclinations and did not typically speak in terms of the original understanding. But in twenty-first-century conservative thought, Frankfurter and Harlan have greatly receded in importance, and originalism has become far more significant, endorsed as it is by Justices Scalia and Thomas, the most prominent conservatives on the Roberts Court.

The second alternative is *conservative heroism*. Conservative heroism is responsible for the attack on affirmative action programs, the effort to strike down restrictions on commercial advertising, gun regulations, and limits on campaign expenditures, and the movement to protect property rights against "regulatory takings." Conservative Heroes are not greatly concerned with the original understanding of the founding document, and they are entirely willing to renovate longstanding practices by reference to ambitious ideas about constitutional liberty.

The most influential members of the *Lochner* Court were of course conservative Heroes, striking down progressive legislation, and many people would like the current justices to resume their work. They refer to "the lost Constitution" or "the Constitution in Exile," and they want it to be rediscovered and reclaimed. Some fans of conservative heroism invoke the original understanding, but it is best to take that link with several grains of salt. Many of the central arguments are based on a heroic effort to infuse the Constitution with what is taken to be the best contemporary moral arguments—not to track the thinking of people long dead. Conservative Heroes often invoke libertarian arguments about economic freedom and want judges to scrutinize federal and state laws by reference to their preferred ideals. In many cases, they are right to object to those laws as a matter of principle. The question is whether judges should listen to their complaints.

What, if anything, unifies Burkean minimalism, originalism, and conservative heroism? The simplest answer is that all three disapprove of those forms of liberal thought that culminated in the work of the Warren Court and on occasion its successors. In short, all three reject liberal heroism. They sharply oppose the idea, prominent in the late 1970s and early 1980s, that the Supreme Court should build on footnote four (the most famous footnote in all of constitutional law) in its 1938 decision in *Carolene Products*, where the Court said this:

> It is unnecessary to consider now whether legislation which restricts those political processes which can ordinarily be expected to bring about repeal of undesirable legislation, is to be subjected to more exacting judicial scrutiny under the general prohibitions of the Fourteenth Amendment than are most other types of legislation. . . .
>
> Nor need we inquire whether similar considerations enter into the review of statutes directed at particular religious . . . or national . . . or racial minorities . . . : whether prejudice against discrete and insular minorities may be a special condition, which tends seriously to curtail the operation of those political processes ordinarily to be relied upon to protect minorities, and which may call for a correspondingly more searching judicial inquiry.

With these words, the Court seemed to make space for both soldiering and heroism and to establish the line between them. According to the footnote, judges should develop constitutional law by reference to a theory of democracy and protect traditionally disadvantaged groups from majoritarian processes. In short, judges should be Soldiers most of the time, but Heroes when self-government is at risk. Burkean Minimalists, originalists, and conservative Heroes do not love that idea.

All three approaches are also skeptical of *Roe v. Wade*, protecting abortion rights; decisions granting various forms of constitutional protection to gays and lesbians; decisions to remove religion from the public sphere; and decisions providing new protections to suspected criminals. It follows that all three approaches are properly characterized as conservative simply because of their shared doubts about the liberal rulings of the Warren Court and the arguments offered by that

[73]

Court's most enthusiastic defenders. But there are massive disagreements as well.

Burkean Minimalists have little interest, for example, in originalism. From the minimalist perspective, originalism is far too radical, and its occasional heroism counts against it; it calls for dramatic movements in the law, changing longstanding understandings, and it is unacceptable for exactly that reason. Burkean Minimalists respect precedent and prize stability, and they are entirely willing to accept decisions that do not comport with the original understanding, simply because a decision to overrule them would disrupt established practices. To Burkean Minimalists, originalism looks uncomfortably close to the French Revolution, seeking to overthrow settled traditions by reference to an abstract theory.

Nor do Burkean Minimalists have any enthusiasm for conservative heroism, which they also consider unacceptably arrogant. To be sure, they are willing to build on existing law through analogical reasoning, and on occasion, this process of building might allow Burkean Minimalists to make common cause with their rationalist adversaries. But insofar as rationalist Minimalists are willing to invoke various accounts (of, say, property rights, presidential power over war-making, or color-blindness), to produce large-scale departures from existing practice and law, Burkean Minimalists have no interest in their enterprise. They trust social practices more than they trust theories, even if those theories are not terribly ambitious. They care about consequences and they dislike abstractions.

NARROW AND SHALLOW

Narrowness. There are different forms of minimalism, but as we saw in chapter 1, all of them share a preference for small steps over large ones. With respect to the war on terror, for example, the Court has favored narrow rulings, refusing to speak broadly about the president's power as commander-in-chief and generally leaving a great deal undecided. In the domain of affirmative action, many of the Court's rulings have been particularistic, arguing that while one program is unacceptable, another one might not be. Or consider the "undue burden" standard, adopted by the Court as a test for whether restrictions on abortion should be upheld. This standard is hardly a clear rule; it calls for close attention to the details of the particular restriction at issue. It invites case-by-case judgments and in that sense exhibits minimalism.

Minimalists fear that wide rulings will produce errors that are at once serious and difficult to reverse—a particular problem when the stakes are high. Hence they insist that narrowness is especially desirable in any period in which national security is seriously threatened. Justice Frankfurter's concurring opinion in the *Steel Seizure Case* offers the most elaborate discussion of the basic point. In that case, the Court ruled against President Truman's claim of authority to seize the nation's steel mills (to maintain production during the Korean War). But several of the Court's members wrote separately. Justice Frankfurter emphasized that "rigorous adherence to the narrow scope of the judicial function" is especially important in constitutional cases when national security is at risk, notwithstanding the country's "eagerness to settle—preferably forever—a specific problem on the basis of the broadest possible constitutional pronouncement." In his view, the Court's duty "lies in the opposite direction," through judgments that make it unnecessary to consider "delicate problems of power under the Constitution." Thus the Court has an obligation "to avoid putting fetters upon the future by needless pronouncements today." Justice Frankfurter concluded that "the issue before us can be met, and therefore should be, without attempting to define the President's powers comprehensively."[1] Justice Frankfurter is arguing for minimalism on the ground that it reduces the risk that mistaken judicial decisions will impose undesirable limits on democratic processes.

In many domains, sensible people take small steps in order to preserve their options, aware as they are that large steps can have unintended bad consequences, particularly if they are difficult to reverse. In law, wide rulings might produce outcomes that judges and the nation as a whole will come to regret. This point derives strength from a special feature of adjudication, which often grows out of particular disputes based on particular facts. Unlike legislators and administrators, judges frequently do not "see" a broad array of fact patterns, suitable for decision by rule. Lacking information about a range of situations, judges are often in a poor position to produce wide rulings. For that reason, they often prefer to be Minimalists.

These are points about the risks and costs of error, but there is an additional problem. For any official, it can be extremely burdensome to generate a wide rule in which it is possible to have much confidence. Narrow decisions might therefore reduce the costs of decision at the same time that they reduce the costs of error.

Shallowness. We have also seen that Minimalists seek rulings that are *shallow rather than deep.* Shallow rulings attempt to produce rationales and outcomes on which diverse people can agree, notwithstanding their disagreement on the most fundamental issues. For example, there are vigorous disputes about the underlying purpose of the free speech guarantee: Should the guarantee be seen as protecting democratic self-government, or the marketplace of ideas, or individual autonomy? Heroes like to think about these questions, but Minimalists don't, and they hope not to answer them. They seek judgments and rulings that can attract shared support from people who are committed to one or another of these foundational understandings, or who are unsure about the foundations of the free speech principle.

The Minimalist's preference for shallowness is rooted in three considerations. First, shallow decisions, no less than narrow ones, reduce the burdens of decision. To say the least, it can be extremely difficult to decide on the foundations of a whole area of constitutional law; shallow rulings make such decisions unnecessary. Second, shallow rulings may prevent errors. A judicial judgment in favor of one or another foundational account may well produce significant mistakes; shallowness is less error-prone, simply by virtue of its agnosticism on the deep issues of the day. If several different foundational accounts, or all reasonable contenders, can converge on a rationale or an outcome, there is good reason to believe that the rationale or outcome is right.

Third, shallow rulings tend to promote social peace at the same time that they show a high degree of respect to those who disagree on large questions. In a heterogeneous society, it is generally good to assure citizens, to the extent possible, that their own deepest commitments have not been ruled off-limits. By accomplishing this task, shallow rulings reduce the intensity of social conflicts and promote a degree of social peace. This practical point is supplemented by a deeper one, which is that those who seek shallowness are demonstrating respect for competing foundational commitments. Those who practice minimalism embrace the idea of civic respect.

In the abstract, of course, narrowness and shallowness may be nothing to celebrate (see chapter 4), and this is why Heroes and Soldiers do not accept minimalism. Here as elsewhere, we need to investigate the costs of decisions and the costs of errors. Narrowness is likely to breed unpredictability and perhaps unequal treatment; it might even do violence to the rule of law, simply because it leaves so much uncertainty. In many contexts, clear rules are preferable to vague, open-ended standards, and it can be worthwhile to risk the breadth and potential crudeness of rules in order to increase clarity, so as to give people a better signal of their rights and obligations. A specified speed limit is a lot better than a requirement that people drive "prudently."

In the areas of contract, tort, and property law, narrowness would be unacceptable, because people require clarity in those domains; you cannot safely enter into contracts, or enjoy the use of your property, unless you have a clear sense of the rules. In many areas of constitutional law, it is important to allow people to plan. Judicial humility is important, to be sure, but it isn't exactly helpful if people have no idea about the nature of free speech rights on the Internet. Narrow rulings reduce the burdens imposed on judges in the case at hand, but they also "export" decision-making duties to others, in a way that can increase those burdens on balance. Insofar as Minimalists prize narrowness, they are vulnerable to challenge on the ground that they leave too much openness in the system. Both Heroes and Soldiers press this point against them.

Shallowness certainly has its virtues. But if a deep theory is correct, maybe judges ought to adopt it. A shallow ruling, one that is agnostic on the right approach to the Constitution, would seem to be a major error if a more ambitious approach, though contentious, is actually correct. Suppose, for example, that a certain theory—of free speech, the president's authority as commander-in-chief, property rights—would produce the right foundation for future development. If so, there is good reason for courts to endorse it. Minimalists might leave uncertainty about the content of the law at the same time that they obscure its roots. Heroes can claim to produce far more in the way of clarity; consider the Court's invocation or ideas about liberty and dignity in 2015, protecting the right to same-sex marriage. I will return to these objections below.

We should also be able to see why minimalism cannot be a complete theory of interpretation. Small steps can go in multiple different directions. A Minimalist can have any number of ideological orientations. A Minimalist could favor small steps in the direction of originalism, or in the direction of moral readings, or in the direction of democracy-reinforcement, or even in the direction of soldiering. In one case after another, a Minimalist might move by increments in the different of their apparent adversaries (including Heroes and Soldiers). Nonetheless, the Minimalist is a distinctive breed. By favoring small, theoretically unambitious opinions, those who endorse minimalism invite serious conflicts with both Heroes and Soldiers.

Practices and Judgments

It is important to distinguish between Burkean minimalism and its more rationalist counterpart. Of course Minimalists prize shallowness; opposition to ambitious theories is part of the defining creed of minimalism. But while all Minimalists favor small steps, rationalists are occasionally skeptical of traditions. They are willing and sometimes even eager to ask whether established practices can survive critical scrutiny.

Rationalist Minimalists also come in many shapes and sizes, but their willingness to reject traditions, and to demand reasons, marks them as non-Burkean or even anti-Burkean. They want justifications, not a history lesson. Burke himself values "prejudice," describing it as "wisdom without reflection, and above it." Rationalists despise that idea.

In 2014, for example, Judge Richard Posner wrote an important opinion for the United States Court of Appeals for the Seventh Circuit, striking down bans on same-sex marriage in Wisconsin and Indiana. Judge Posner thought that the bans had no justification. To the states' (hapless) efforts to defend them, his response was simple: "Go figure." The opinion was mostly heroic; Judge Posner wrote in bold and ambitious terms. But his opinion also had minimalist features insofar as it paid close attention to its existing precedents and attempted to build from them. Whether heroic or minimalist, its thrust was rationalist and anti-Burkean insofar as it ridiculed the idea that the traditional definition of marriage deserved respect simply because it was long-standing. The rationalist Minimalist has no problem asking government: *What have you got to say for yourself?*

This difference between Burkean and rationalist minimalism should not be overstated. No real-world Minimalist is likely to accept all traditions as such; that would be extreme. No real-world Minimalist is likely to want to subject many traditions to critical scrutiny, certainly not at the same time. Any such effort would quickly produce a departure from minimalism in the direction of heroism. In practice, there is a continuum from more Burkean to more rationalist forms of minimalism. But it is nonetheless important to distinguish between the two sets of Minimalists, if only because of their different emphases, which can lead in radically different directions. Consider the question of sex discrimination, where Burkean Minimalists have been inclined to allow governments to do what they want (and thus make common cause with Soldiers), and rationalist Minimalists have demanded a justification (and thus make common cause with Heroes).

As it applies to the judiciary, we can understand Burkean minimalism in two different ways. First, Burkeans might stress actual social *practices*, and see those practices, as they extend over time, as bearing on the proper interpretation of the Constitution. A practice-oriented Burkean would be reluctant to invoke a particular conception of the separation of powers to strike down actions that are longstanding—say, foreign surveillance by the president, or recess appointments by the president when an office is open, or presidential war-making without congressional authorization.

On this view, judges in constitutional cases should follow a distinctive conception of the role of common law judges, which is to respect and mimic, rather than to evaluate, time-honored practices. For such Burkeans, ambiguous constitutional provisions should be understood by reference to such practices, and judges should be reluctant to allow litigants to challenge them. In that event, Burkean Minimalists could make common cause with Soldiers. Indeed, and more ambitiously, judges might even question democratic initiatives that reject longstanding traditions without very good reason. In that event, Burkean Minimalists could again make common cause with Heroes.

Second, and very different, Burkean Minimalists might stress not *social* practices but the slow evolution of *judicial* doctrine over time—and therefore reject sharp breaks from the judiciary's own past. For such Burkeans, what is particularly important is the judiciary's prior judgments, which should in turn be based on a series of small steps and should avoid radical departures. On this view, current judges should respect those prior judgments.

There are large differences between an approach that focuses on social practices and one that focuses on judicial decisions. Those who emphasize practices would be skeptical of evolutionary movements in constitutional law *if* those movements depend on the judges' own moral or political judgments, minimalist though they might be. For Burkeans who emphasize social practices, it is not legitimate for judges to build constitutional law through small steps that reflect the Court's own judgments over time. But for those who see the case-by-case evolution of judge-made constitutional law as an acceptably minimalist project, judicial steps deserve respect, especially in light of the fact that those steps are unlikely to depart radically from public convictions.

Burke Himself

Burke himself emphasized social practices rather than judicial judgments, but he tended to collapse the two (which is interesting in its own right, because it suggests a distinctive view of law). I do not attempt anything like an exegesis of Burke, an exceedingly complex figure, in this space, but let us turn briefly to Burke himself and in particular to his great essay on the French Revolution, in which he rejected the revolutionary temperament because of its theoretical ambition.[2] We can see Burke's essay as a thoroughgoing attack on the Persona of the Hero in politics.

Burke's key claim is that the "science of constructing a commonwealth, or reforming it, is, like every other experimental science, not to be taught a priori." To make this argument, Burke opposes theories and abstractions, developed by individual minds, to traditions, built up by many minds over long periods. In his most vivid passage, Burke writes:

> We wished at the period of the Revolution, and do now wish, to derive all we possess as *an inheritance from our forefathers.* . . . The science of government being therefore so practical in itself, and intended for such practical purposes, a matter which requires experience, and even more experience than any person can gain in his whole life, however sagacious and observing he may be, it is with infinite caution than any man ought to venture upon pulling down an edifice which has answered in any tolerable degree, for ages the common purposes of society, or on building it up again, without having models and patterns of approved utility before his eyes.

Thus Burke stresses the need to rely on experience and in particular the experience of generations; and he objects to "pulling down an edifice," a metaphor capturing the understanding of social practices as reflecting the judgments of numerous people extending over time. It is for this reason that Burke describes the "spirit of innovation"—which Heroes tend to admire—as "the result of a selfish temper and confined views," and goes so far as offer the term "prejudice" as one of enthusiastic approval, noting that "instead of casting away all our old prejudices, we cherish them to a very considerable degree." Emphasizing the critical importance of stability, Burke adds a reference to "the evils of inconstancy and versatility, ten thousand times worse than those of obstinacy and the blindest prejudice."

Burke's sharpest distinction, then, is between established practices and individual reason. He contends that wise citizens, aware of their own limitations, will effectively delegate decision-making authority to their own traditions. "We are afraid to put men to live and trade each on his own private stock of reason," simply "because we suspect that this stock in each man is small, and that the individuals would do better to avail themselves of the general bank and capital of nations, and of ages. Many of our men of speculation, instead of exploding general prejudices, employ their sagacity to discover the latent wisdom which prevails in them."

To be sure, it would be possible to object to Burke's argument on the ground that some traditions are a product not of wisdom or widespread agreement, but something far less assuring, such as a collective action problem, in which individuals, though unhappy about those traditions, are unable to organize themselves to correct them. (Consider women under conditions of widespread inequality.[3]) Or traditions may persist as a result of significant disparities in power and authority, as some people (whites? religious minorities? the able-bodied?) are able to insist on practices that other people (African Americans? religious minorities? the disabled?) despise. Or traditions may become entrenched as a result of social cascade, in which people simply imitate other people. These are important objections to Burkeanism in all its forms,[4] and Heroes are especially drawn to them. For present purposes, the only point is that if many independent judgments have been made on behalf of a social practice, there is a real argument in favor of adopting a presumption in its favor.

In light of his basic argument, we might expect Burke to express some skepticism about judge-made common law, treating it as a form of a priori intervention by unaccountable judges whose decisions are not rooted in actual experience. But as noted in chapter 1, Burke sees his claims as a reason to value rather than to repudiate the common law, which he goes so far as to call the "pride of the human intellect." On his view, the common law is best taken as a reflection, rather than as a repudiation, of traditions.

Burke goes so far as to contend that "with all its defects, redundancies, and errors," jurisprudence counts as "the collected reason of ages, combining the principles of original justice with the infinite variety of human concerns." Of course jurisprudence lacks a simple, unitary theory, and it was hardly constructed a priori; but it is a product of experience, which is its signal virtue, and which Minimalists prize. Burke appears to be seeing the common law as a form of customary law, developing with close reference to actual practices, which it tends to codify.

On this view, theoretical attacks on the common law—such as those based on utilitarianism—show far too much confidence in an abstract theory, and far too little respect for the collective wisdom of entrenched practices. Here is where Burke most departs from heroism, seeing it as dangerous. Something similar might be said of some areas of constitutional law, in which a committed Burkean might distrust judge-made theoretical abstractions in favor of the occasionally unruly and apparently self-contradictory social practices that are built on the basis of particulars. At the same time, some Burkeans might be willing to celebrate American constitutional law, which might be regarded as collected reason as well, combining principles with infinitely various human concerns.[5]

Burke and Judicial Review

Burke did not, of course, develop an account of judicial review. English courts lacked (and lack) the power to strike down legislation, and hence it could not possibly have occurred to Burke to explore the nature and limits of that power. Indeed, Burkeans might be tempted to reject judicial review altogether, perhaps on the ground that judges are too likely to go off on larks of their own. Perhaps little revolutions, of the kind if not on the scale that Burke despised, are a predictable product of an independent judiciary entrusted with the power to invalidate the outcomes of democratic processes. Some Burkeans might want to be good Soldiers, insistent on upholding those outcomes.

But for those who sympathize with Burke's arguments, a Burkean account of judicial review is not difficult to sketch. The central point is that courts ought to protect time-honored practices against democratic renovations based on theories, or passions, that show an insufficient appreciation for those practices. The goal would be to provide a safeguard against the revolutionary or even purely rationalistic spirit in democratic legislatures. One way to put it is that the goal would be to target, and to squelch, political Heroes, at least if they attempt to override traditions. Another way to put it is that the goal of some Burkeans would be to make common cause with Heroes insofar as they attempt to protect traditions against democratic override. By protecting traditions, Burkeans could, in a sense, count as Heroes. We will see both of these themes.

Nor are these ideas at all foreign to American constitutional law. The Constitution's due process clause forbids governments from depriving people of life, liberty, or property "without due process of law." But what does that mean? The clause has long been understood in terms of traditions. In his dissenting opinion in *Lochner*, Justice Holmes, though not at all Burkean, struck an unmistakably Burkean chord when he wrote that the clause would be violated if "a rational and fair man necessarily would admit that the statute proposed would infringe fundamental principles *as they have been understood by the traditions of our people and our law*." Holmes wanted to limit the reach of the courts—he was a Soldier—but he agreed that if a law would interfere with basic principles as understood by traditions, the courts should strike it down under the due process clause.

Or consider the incorporation doctrine, which has led the Court to rule that most provisions of the Bill of Rights, which originally applied only to the federal government, also apply to the states, because they are "incorporated in" the Fourteenth Amendment. As the Court's decisions were written, the incorporation rulings had a great deal to do with Burkean thinking, especially insofar as Justice Frankfurter played a significant role. Thus Justice Frankfurter explicitly urged that in deciding whether the actions of states have violated the Constitution, courts should ask whether those actions "offend those canons of decency and fairness which express the notions of justice of English-speaking peoples." And in the end, the Court has resolved the question whether a provision of the original Bill of Rights applies to the states by inquiring whether it "is necessary to an Anglo-American regime of ordered liberty." Of course it would be possible to understand "ordered liberty" in heroic or purely theoretical terms. But in the account that Justice Frankfurter spurred, the focus was on "an Anglo-American regime," which placed the spotlight squarely on identifiable traditions.

Or consider modern "substantive due process," by which the Court understands the due process clause not merely to protect fair procedures, but also to safeguard individual rights as such. Which rights? The Court has often answered that question with close reference to tradition. Many of the key decisions have asked about certain kinds of privacy—for example, whether people have a constitutional right to use contraceptives, to live with their family members, to engage in same-sex sexual activity, or to physician-assisted suicide. Justice Harlan's approach, which has influenced the Court for decades, was based on "continual insistence upon respect for the teachings of history, solid recognition of the values that underlie our society."

Of course some Heroes strenuously disagree, contending that rights evolve and grow, and thinking instead that judges should ask which rights really are fundamental, not which rights have been recognized by history. In recognizing the right to same-sex marriage, the Court emphasized "the right of all persons as we learn its meaning." The Court's heroic opinion, emphasizing "new insight," is a clear rejection of Burkeanism.

Some justices have insisted that unless a claimed right can claim firm roots in tradition, courts should not intervene to protect it. In rejecting the right to physician-assisted suicide, the Court said that substantive due process has been "carefully refined by concrete examples involving fundamental rights found to be deeply rooted in our legal tradition." The Court claimed that this approach "tends to rein in the subjective elements" and "avoids the need for complex balancing" in particular cases by fallible judges. Thus the Court's inquiry was framed by asking "whether this asserted right has any place in our Nation's tradition." On this highly Burkean view, growing out of Holmes's dissenting opinion in *Lochner*, the Court should not strike down legislation merely because it offends the judges' account of reason or justice, or even because it is inconsistent with evolving or current social norms. To cabin would-be Heroes, potentially embarking on larks of their own, it is necessary also to show a violation of principles that are at once long-standing and deeply held. When the Court said that public officials could not ban members of a family from living with one another (*Moore v. City of East Cleveland*), it could make a plausible Burkean argument, rooted in traditions of respect for family living arrangements.

Of course the Court has often refused to follow this Burkean approach to the due process clause, in a way that has sharply divided Burkean Minimalists on the one hand from rationalist Minimalists and Heroes on the other. When the Court recognized the right to choose abortion in *Roe v. Wade*, it could not claim a reliable basis in tradition, and the same is true for the Court's ruling that the due process clause creates a right to same-sex marriage.

Shields and Swords

This latter point clarifies the need to make a distinction between two kinds of Burkean decisions: those that uphold and those that invalidate democratic judgments.

Burkean minimalism can operate as a shield or a sword. Insofar as it operates as a shield, it protects the decisions of democratic processes from the courts. In such cases, Burkean Minimalists make common cause with Soldiers. Consider, for example, the idea that courts should uphold prohibitions on same-sex marriage or restrictions on campaign expenditures. But insofar as Burkean minimalism operates as a sword, it attacks decisions that emerge from democratic processes. In such cases, Burkean Minimalists become aligned with Heroes. Consider, for example, the idea that courts should strike down restrictions on property rights or on freedom of religion.

By their very nature, committed Burkeans should be sympathetic to efforts, by state and federal governments, to defend their own time-honored practices against constitutional attack. If states are attempting to regulate obscenity, to prevent gambling, or to depart from the idea of one person, one vote, their decisions might be supported on Burkean grounds. Many people have invoked Burkean arguments to defend restrictions on obscenity; rationalists disagree, contending that such restrictions have no point. And when government is acting in a way that seems to favor one kind of religious belief, Burkeans should not object *if* that form of favoritism has clear support in longstanding social traditions. Here, then, is a real split between Burkean Minimalists and their rational cousins, who are far more willing to strike down any kind of favoritism for particular religions or even for religion as such.

Consider, for example, the question whether there is a convincing constitutional objection to the words "under God" in the Pledge of Allegiance. Strikingly, Chief Justice Rehnquist's defense of the use of those words was an almost entirely Burkean exercise, stressing practices rather than reasons for practices. Indeed, Chief Justice Rehnquist's view of the establishment clause has a persistent Burkean feature, at least insofar as he would permit public recognition of God—as, for example, in high school ceremonies—by reference not to theories or principle, but to history alone. By contrast, *Brown v. Board of Education*, invalidating racial segregation, and *Frontiero v. Richardson*, striking down sex discrimination, cannot easily be defended on strictly Burkean grounds—even though rationalist Minimalists might well approve of them as building incrementally on judicial precedents.

The separation of powers might be understood in similar terms. When a current president is engaging in an action in which presidents have long engaged, and with congressional acquiescence, Burkean Minimalists would be strongly inclined to uphold that action. The central point is more general. If Burkean minimalism operates as a shield to be used on government's behalf, we could easily imagine an endorsement, by many Burkeans, of a kind of tradition-based soldiering—on the theory that decisions about whether to change longstanding practices should be made democratically, not by judges at all. On the Burkean view, judges should be most reluctant to use the Constitution to undertake any kind of reform. Burkeans do not want any echo of the French Revolution, however quiet it might seem.

Now turn to the use of Burkeanism as a sword. If a government is dramatically altering longstanding practices or the status quo, Burkeanism might be invoked as the basis for attacking the attempted alteration. We have seen that the due process clause has been so invoked in cases involving familial privacy, where the Court has claimed that government intrusions on that value are inconsistent with national traditions. There are analog in other domains, where established traditions have also helped to convince courts to impose limits on what government may do. In striking down an unusual Colorado law that prohibited gays and lesbians from obtaining local antidiscrimination measures, the Court said, "It is not within our constitutional tradition to enact laws of this sort." Whether or not the Court's argument was convincing, it is noteworthy that the majority saw fit to invoke tradition.

Burke and Rational Criticism of Traditions

Rationalist Minimalists seek narrowness and shallowness, but they are entirely willing to scrutinize traditions and established practices. An underlying idea is that traditions are sometimes unjust and that society frequently progresses by subjecting them to serious challenge—and that constitutional law is a legitimate part of that enterprise. On this view, the delegation of decision-making authority to longstanding traditions is perverse, and Burke was quite wrong to treat "prejudice" as a word of approval. Rationalist Minimalists are not willing to be Heroes, but they are willing to march with them, at least on occasion.

Return to the long series of decisions striking down discrimination on the basis of sex. In those decisions, the Court did not act abruptly; it built up the doctrine by small, incompletely theorized steps. But it could not claim to rest on traditions. On the contrary, the sex discrimination cases squarely reject Burkeanism by repeatedly opposing "reasoned analysis" to "traditional, often inaccurate, assumptions about the proper roles of men and women" and to the "accidental byproduct of a traditional way of thinking about females"—with the suggestion that laws that are "accidental byproducts" are unconstitutional for that very reason. Tradition serves in these cases as a term of opprobrium, not praise. Indeed, the Court has struck down sex discrimination on the express ground that it is a product of habit and tradition, rather than reason, and it has required government to defend any such discrimination in terms that Burkeans would find puzzling at best.

Nor can Burkeanism account for the Court's decisions establishing the right to vote, including the one-person, one-vote rule and even *Bush v. Gore*. The Court's voting rights doctrines were developed by increments, with *Bush v. Gore* explicitly noting its own minimalism—but the Court hardly built on traditions. Indeed, many people originally challenged the one-person, one-vote rule on heavily Burkean grounds, with the suggestion that the Court was allowing a contentious theory to override longstanding practices at the state level. (Note that the composition of the US Senate violates the one-person, one-vote rule.)

The Court's decision in *Lawrence v. Texas*, striking down the ban on same-sex sodomy, is an excellent illustration of rationalist minimalism. In *Lawrence*, the Court did not and could not claim that its decision was securely rooted in longstanding traditions. Bans on same-sex relations are (unfortunately) part of national traditions. On the contrary, the

Court emphasized an *"emerging awareness* that liberty gives substantial protection to adult persons in deciding how to conduct their private lives in matters pertaining to sex." Hence the Court looked forward to what was now emerging, not backward to what was long settled. In the Court's view, what was emerging was a product of sense and hard-won wisdom rather than arrogance or hubris. In cases involving protection of gays and lesbians, rationalist minimalism has been the coin of the realm (and in the case of same-sex marriage, a dose of heroism).

In many areas, the Supreme Court has acted incrementally, in common law fashion, but in a way that is sharply critical of traditions and that looks forward to a constitutionally preferred future. Indeed, much of equal protection doctrine is forward-looking in this sense, rooted as it is in a principle of equality that operates as a challenge to longstanding practices. In its modest forms, this is a form of rationalist minimalism, demanding reasons and forbidding "animus" against disabled people or gays and lesbians.

With respect to religious liberty, establishment clause doctrine has a similar feature, with history often creating problems for the Court's attempt to elaborate a theory of religious neutrality, which history does not support. After all, the United States is, in many respects, a Christian nation, as its traditions reflect. The Court's theory of neutrality cannot claim firm roots in those traditions. Justice Stevens, a rationalist as well as a frequent Minimalist, insisted, as against those who focus on "our heritage," that judges must apply "the broad principles that the Framers wrote ... by expounding the meaning of constitutional provisions with one eye towards our Nation's history and the other fixed on its democratic aspirations."

In the context of the equal protection clause, I believe that rationalist minimalism has large advantages over its Burkean sibling, as I will explain shortly. For the moment, however, my goal is to see how the two sides differ, and how they might engage with one another.

Traditions in Packages?

At this stage the very distinction between Burkean and rationalist minimalism might be challenged on the ground that traditions do not come in neat packages for judicial identification. Traditions are hardly self-defining, and this point might seem to complicate the Burkean enterprise.

When a court attempts to follow a tradition, what, exactly, is it supposed to follow? Should a tradition be characterized at a high level of generality—involving, say, respect for intimate personal choices? Or should it be described at a low level—allowing, say, government interference with such choices when traditional morality is being violated? Or suppose that circumstances have changed—as a result, for example, of the rise of terrorism. If so, how should we characterize an apparent "tradition" of limited presidential prerogatives? Might not any such characterization have an evaluative element, and not be a simple matter of finding something?

Perhaps Burkeans must ultimately turn out to be rationalists, in the sense that they must themselves offer their own particular account of tradition, based on their "private stock of reason." On this view, any characterization of a tradition will have to be "interpretive," in Dworkin's sense that it must be a matter not of simply finding something, but of placing longstanding practices in what judges deem to be a sensible light. In the long arc of American constitutional law, many people have thought that traditions should be read at a high level of generality, so as to contain certain abstractions ("the right to engage in consensual sexual activities" or "the right to choose your own spouse"). These abstractions might then be used to test, and find wanting, particular practices, even longstanding ones. If traditions are so used, changes might be sought not in spite of traditions but in their name. If so, the distinction between Burkean and rationalist minimalism begins to vanish. For this reason, the Burkean approach might have an inevitable rationalist dimension, one that is obscured by traditionalist talk.

But committed Burkeans have several responses. First, they might bite the bullet, acknowledge this point, and urge simply that their Burkeanism is fully consistent with it. Burke himself believed that traditions were far from static. His claim was that social change should emerge from traditions, not in opposition to them. If this is the central point, the line between Burkean and rationalist minimalism does become a lot thinner, if only because reason will have to be used in deciding what kind of change should occur—a major concession to rationalists.

But perhaps we can thicken the relevant line. Perhaps Burkeans will want to adopt a (soldierly) presumption in favor of democratic outcomes—an inclination that divides Justice Frankfurter, who adopted such a presumption, from Justice O'Connor, who did not. On this view, the best understanding of Burkean minimalism ensures that courts *will rarely strike down legislation unless that legislation is palpably inconsistent with traditions or defies the unmistakable lessons of experience.* Sure, change can occur, and traditions can be revised, but through democratic rather than judicial judgments. On this view, the difference between Burkean and rationalist Minimalists is that members of the latter group are far more willing to invoke their own moral and political arguments to invalidate legislation. Burkeans are more likely to behave like Soldiers.

Second, Burkeans might insist on reading traditions at a low level of abstraction, in a way that will sharpen the distinction from rationalist Minimalists by eliminating the theory-building and tradition-characterizing duties of the judiciary. Through this approach, Burkeans again might become more soldierly. Justice Scalia, emphasizing deference to tradition, points to the need to consider "the most specific level at which a relevant tradition protecting, or denying protection to, the asserted right can be identified." This approach expressly denies judges the power "to consult and if possible reason from, the traditions . . . in general."[6] By rejecting that power, and by distrusting

[93]

the effort to "reason from" tradition, Justice Scalia is squarely embracing a Burkean approach to the role of the Court in constitutional cases; he is reading the due process clause so as to delegate authority to the tradition, rather than to authorize judges to use tradition as a foundation for evaluative arguments of their own.

If we agree that traditions should be read at a low level of abstraction, then it is genuinely possible to follow them, rather than to characterize them. For that reason, the difference between Burkean Minimalists and their rationalist siblings is real. It should be apparent that insofar as Burkean Minimalists adopt either a (soldierly) presumption in favor of democratic processes or insist on reading traditions at a high level of generality, they become a bit less minimalist, simply because they reject narrowness in constitutional doctrine and begin to convert the doctrine into a system of rules.

ORIGINALISTS AND BURKEANS

In chapter 2, we saw that no approach to constitutional law makes sense in every imaginable context. In our world, the strongest objection to originalism is that it would greatly unsettle existing rights and institutions, in a way that would make American constitutional law much worse rather than better. Burkean Minimalists reject originalism for that reason; they believe that originalists are in the grip of an abstract theory, one that would do away with a kind of inheritance. That inheritance takes the form of numerous judicial judgments over long periods of time, in which public commitments, social learning, and desirable adaptation have occasionally led to constitutional rulings that diverge from the original understanding.

Often Minimalists, Burkean and otherwise, contend that this process of evolution was itself anticipated by the founding generation, which did not attempt to freeze its particular views. For this reason, they contend that originalism is self-defeating: The original understanding rejects originalism itself. But that is a contentious historical claim, and Burkeans do not need to make it.

Burke's Counsel

When Burkeans recoil at the suggestion that the founding document should be understood to mean what it originally meant, they are embracing a conception of the Constitution as evolving in the same way as traditions and the common law—not through the idiosyncratic judgments of individual judges, but through a process in which social norms and practices play the key role. It is in this vein that Justice Frankfurter contended, "It is an inadmissibly narrow conception of American constitutional law to confine it to the words of the Constitution and to disregard the gloss which life has written upon them."[7]

Consider, for example, the question whether a congressional declaration of war is a necessary precursor to the use of force by the president—in Afghanistan, in Iraq, in Syria, in Ukraine, or wherever force might be considered. On the basis of the constitutional text, read in light of its history, there is a more than plausible argument that a congressional declaration is indeed necessary. The argument is controversial, but let us simply stipulate that according to the original understanding, the president may not use military force without a congressional declaration of war (at least if the president does not need to respond to a sudden attack).

On strictly Burkean grounds, judicial insistence on a congressional declaration runs into a serious problem: Since the founding, the United States has been involved in more than two hundred armed conflicts, and Congress has declared war on only five occasions! Longstanding practices are inconsistent with the original understanding, and Burkeans insist that those practices must operate as a "gloss" on the document.

At a minimum, Burkeans will notice that a congressional authorization to use military force (called an "AUMF") has often operated as the functional equivalent of a declaration of war, and they will contend that such an authorization gives the president the same power that is accorded by a declaration. But Burkeans will add that if the president has often used force with neither a declaration nor an authorization, constitutional law must give some attention to that fact—and at least consider the possibility that for some kinds of military actions (perhaps short-term ones, not amounting to "war"), congressional authorization is not required at all. The example could easily be extended to many cases in which social practices and judicial decisions have outrun the original understanding. Here as elsewhere, Burkeans distrust Heroes, originalist or otherwise.

An important example involves the president's power to make recess appointments. Consider an important if highly technical question: Is "the Recess" (in the words of the Constitution) limited to the *intersession* recess, which occurs between two-year congressional sessions, or can it include *intrasession* recesses, which occur when Congress takes breaks ("recesses") amid sessions? In terms of the original understanding, there is a strong argument that "the Recess" meant only the intersession recess. To be sure, the question is not straightforward. There is some linguistic ambiguity. The term "the Recess" is not exactly clear. Apart from the ambiguity of the term, the intersession-only interpretation is severely complicated by the fact that intrasession recesses *did not even occur until after the Civil War.* We cannot know that "the" meant "the one and only" when intrasession recesses did not exist.

In those circumstances, the original public meaning of "the Recess" is not self-evident. Perhaps the ratifiers would have agreed that "the Recess" includes any protracted period in which Congress is not in session, and perhaps that is enough to introduce ambiguity. On originalist premises, the answer can be disputed. But at least we should acknowledge that when the Constitution was ratified, "the Recess" was understood to refer to the intersession recess.

In these circumstances, the Burkean's counsel is simple: The Court should be reluctant to adopt a contested understanding of the text to override longstanding understandings on the part of the president and the Senate alike. In the case of the words "the Recess," it appears that at least since 1921, their shared understanding included intra-session recesses. Burkeans would give a lot of weight to that shared understanding.

With respect to recess appointments, it is also disputed whether the constitutional requirement that a recess must "happen" during the recess means that it must *arise* during that time, or whether it is sufficient if it *exists* during that time. Suppose, for example, that the office of secretary of state becomes vacant while the Senate is in session, but that it is not filled during that time, and that the Senate then goes on recess. May the president make a recess appointment of a new secretary of state? If we insist on following the text and the original understanding, we might well conclude that "happen" means "arise"—and hence that the president cannot make a recess appointment under those circumstances. But the Burkean, calling attention to longstanding traditions, will emphasize that since 1823, presidents have understood "happen" to mean "exist," and the Senate does not appear to have disagreed with that understanding.

Here as well, the Burkean will find the longstanding practice of overwhelming importance. And indeed the Supreme Court, in a highly Burkean opinion by Justice Breyer, did exactly that in 2014—over the predictably heated dissent of Justice Scalia. Justice Breyer wrote unambiguously, "in interpreting the Clause, we put significant weight upon historical practice."

Against Disruption, against Heroes

In such disputes, the strongest Burkean point, against originalism, involves the risks associated with wholesale disruption of contemporary political life and constitutional law, including understandings of rights and institutions on which many Americans have come to rely. (At least this is so if originalism is understood to require fidelity to the originally expected applications of a provision; as we have seen, some originalists take some constitutional provisions to set out broad terms whose meaning changes over time.) Heroes are fine with disruption; they might even like it. By contrast, disruption is exactly what Burkeans hope to avoid.

In the domain of national institutions, the Court's willingness to allow independent regulatory agencies, operating outside of the direct control of the president, is the simplest example. Recall that independent agencies include the National Labor Relations Board, the Federal Communications Commission, the Federal Trade Commission, and the Securities and Exchange Commission. Are such agencies unconstitutional? Can Congress really immunize such important parts of the government from the control of the president?

The historical question is disputed, because the eighteenth-century record is unclear. But there is at least a plausible argument that purely as a matter of the original understanding, Congress lacked the authority to create such independent agencies—and that implementation of the laws had to occur under the authority of the president. But a dramatic departure from the current system, striking down the independence of such agencies, would unsettle much of American government. It would throw established institutions into great disarray. Burkeans do not want to do that.

In the domain of rights, there are prominent examples as well, including the rule of one person, one vote and the prohibition on school prayer. A decision to revisit these rulings would threaten deeply entrenched features of American constitutional law. Notwithstanding their occasional heroism and their dubious Burkean roots, many of the rights-protecting decisions of the Warren and Burger Courts have now become embedded in national life. Burkeans believe that there is good reason to respect entrenched decisions, even if they were not necessarily legitimate when they were initially issued.

To be sure, they might be more open to efforts to revisit judicial decisions than practices on which the president and Congress have converged. But Burkeans are skeptical about the whole idea of disruption, especially when it is undertaken in the name of the large-scale theory, and when it purports to be heroic. Consistent Burkeans distrust Heroes even if the practices that they seek to invalidate initially lacked a good Burkean pedigree.

Heroes and Burkeans

No responsible Hero believes that judges can legitimately create the Constitution anew; their job involves interpretation, not rewriting (see chapter 2). Hence judges owe a duty of fidelity to text, precedent, and all other relevant sources of law. But to the extent that fidelity permits, Heroes believe that judges are entitled and even required to develop high-level principles that make sense out of an area of law.

Suppose, for example, that the best way to make moral sense of the takings clause (which protects against government takings of private property) is to offer very strong protection to property rights. If so, heroic judges might well conclude that the Court should adopt that view, even if the result is to strike down a lot of legislation. Or suppose that the best way to make sense of the free speech clause is to emphasize the importance of individual autonomy—the right to say what you like, when you like, and as you like. If so, then Heroes favor that understanding to the extent that it can be made to fit with existing law. As a result, some Heroes have said that the Constitution protects any and all obscenity (with the possible exception of child pornography), and others have said that it protects blanket protection to libel, and still others have insisted that it provides broad protection to commercial advertising, treating it as essentially equivalent to political dissent.

With respect to the fourth amendment, Heroes are inclined to question many practices with respect to surveillance. They believe that much of what is and has been done, by the Central Intelligence Agency and the National Security Agency, raises serious constitutional problems. On these counts, many rationalist Minimalists would be prepared to make common cause with Heroes. They would favor small steps, but they might well move in the direction that Heroes favor.

By contrast, Burkeans distrust abstract or a priori reasoning, and hence they will be deeply skeptical of any approach of this sort. In their view, Heroes make a big mistake, which is to underestimate their own propensity to blunder, not least when they are developing high-level principles or attempting to decide what makes best moral sense. On this count, Burkeans invoke Justice Holmes's cautionary note about "the accident" of whether we find certain views familiar or instead shocking. Burkeans stress that Heroes are especially prone to error if they deploy their own moral convictions as a weapon against democratic processes, and if they have not acted with close reference to actual practices, existing norms, and case-by-case reasoning. They are most uncomfortable with the view that judges should invoke abstract ideas about liberty or equality as antidemocratic swords.

For them, *Brown v. Board of Education* might be acceptable insofar as it could be seen not as a bolt from the blue, but as the culmination of a long series of decisions and as reflective of a growing social consensus. By contrast, *Roe v. Wade* was, to Burkeans, unacceptably heroic, because it could not be defended in those terms. In *Roe*, the Court ruled quite broadly in its first encounter with the abortion question, and it used a theory of autonomy far too expansively. (Rationalist Minimalists agree, and I think that they are right.) The same is true of *Citizens United* and other heroic efforts to use the First Amendment as the basis for large-scale attacks on campaign finance legislation.

For same-sex marriage, the lesson is plain. Burkeans would oppose a heroic decision in (say) 1960, 1970, 1980, 1990, 2000, or even 2010, if

that decision would have required states to recognize same-sex marriages. But as lower-court decisions accreted, and social norms began
to change, some Burkean judges might become interested in making
common cause with the Hero—and very possibly in ruling that bans
on same-sex marriage offend the Constitution. Of course a rationalist
Minimalist would be willing to consider so ruling. For the rationalist,
the problem is that it is exceedingly hard to identify a legitimate reason
for prohibitions on same-sex marriage. For the Burkean, the argument
would be a harder sell, but a faithful Burkean might not, at a certain
point, consider such a ruling out of bounds—at least if the Court built
carefully on its own precedents and paid careful attention to evolving
social norms. And indeed, that is a fair reading of what the Court did
in 2015, even if it also spoke heroically about liberty and dignity.

Certainly the argument for heroism, and the attack on the most
cautious forms of Burkeanism, would be strengthened if we were
entitled to have real confidence in the theory-building capacities of
federal judges. (See chapter 2.) Even then, the argument would not
be airtight. Those who embrace democracy might object that any
form of heroism would threaten the right of We the People to engage
in self-government. Burkeans might also worry that Heroes would
encounter serious pragmatic problems. By attempting to engraft their
preferred theories onto actual societies, judicial efforts might turn out
to be futile or counterproductive, simply because societies would resist
those efforts. (Recall Bickel's praise of the passive virtues.) But if a theory that fits our practices is indeed appealing in principle, and if heroic
courts can elaborate and implement it, perhaps they should do so.

It is here, of course, that Burkean Minimalists depart from Heroes.
Because they are Minimalists, they distrust theoretical ambition as
such. They lack confidence in judges who enlist large theoretical claims;
in the Burkean view, such judges suffer from hubris. To the extent that
judges are entrusted with power, it is because of their willingness and
ability to elaborate the Constitution's text, read in light of society's

traditions and practices. Whether Heroes are concerned to vindicate their own preferred theory of property rights, or a democratic conception of the free speech principle, or the abstract ideal of human dignity, or their favorite conception of the separation of powers, the Burkean Minimalist firmly opposes them.

BURKEANS AND RATIONALISTS: ARE WE THE ANCIENTS?

Suppose that we are trying to decide between the two forms of minimalism: Burkean and rationalist. On what assumptions should we choose the former? Much of the answer depends on whether Burke was right. If established traditions reflect wisdom rather than accident and force, the argument for Burkean minimalism gains force. Maybe a state wants to ban obscene material; maybe authors of such material object that existing constitutional doctrine can be understood to establish a principle of individual autonomy, one that does not permit government to ban adults from reading and viewing whatever they want. If we believe that the traditional practice, authorizing the ban, is likely to embody wisdom, we might want courts to uphold it, whatever the ideal of individual autonomy seems to require.

In the same vein, Burkeans would want the Court to permit "ceremonial deism," in the form of public recognition of God (as, for example, at a graduation ceremony at a public university). When a constitutional challenge is raised against it, Burkeans reject the challenge largely by reference to traditions. The same analysis would suggest that when initially confronted with the issue, courts should have not have insisted on fidelity to the one-person, one-vote rule. Burkean Minimalists want courts to try to avoid the "political thicket," not because they believe in judicial abstinence as such, but because they think that established practices of political representation deserve respect even if it is not easy to produce a theory to defend them. Speaking of morality generally, ethicist Leon Kass contends that in some domains, "we intuit and feel, immediately and without argument, the violation of things that we rightfully hold dear."⁸ For those who believe that judges ought not to challenge what "we intuit and feel, immediately and without argument," Burkean minimalism has considerable appeal.

As we have seen, rationalist Minimalists are willing to listen to the claim that in some domains, the Court ought to call traditions to account, and should be willing to generalize, from its own precedents, principles that operate as a sharp constraint on government. *Brown v. Board of Education* may have been a hard case for a Burkean, but not so hard for a rationalist. As we have seen, the ban on sex discrimination emerged from this process of generalization. In that context in particular, it is difficult to defend the view that longstanding practices reflect wisdom and sense rather than power and oppression. Some theories of the establishment clause produce sharp critiques of longstanding practices, such as compulsory school prayer and religious ceremonies at Christmastime; those theories are based on requirements of government neutrality that jeopardize a number of traditions that seem to compromise religious liberty. Rationalist Minimalists are willing to strike down government practices by reference to such requirements of neutrality.

Mostly a Soldier, Justice Holmes can also be seen as an originator of a Burkean approach to the due process clause, but he was far more pragmatist than Burkean: "It is revolting to have no better reason for a rule of law than that so it was laid down in the time of Henry IV. It is still more revolting if the grounds upon which it was laid down have vanished long since, and the rule simply persists from blind imitation of the past."⁹ Recall that in his *Lochner* dissent, Holmes insisted that "the accident of our finding certain opinions natural and familiar or novel and even shocking ought not to conclude our judgment upon the question whether statutes embodying them conflict with the Constitution of the United States." Holmes's key point, a deeply anti-Burkean one, is that whether we find opinions "natural and familiar" is itself an "accident" of our time and place. There could be no clearer rejection of Burke's suggestion that our "prejudices" are a reflection not of accident but of hard-won wisdom.

The first paragraph of *The Federalist, No. 1* offers the following contrast: "It has been frequently remarked that it seems to have been reserved to the people of this country, by their conduct and example, to decide the important question, whether societies of men are really capable or not of establishing good government from reflection and choice, or whether they are forever destined to depend for their political constitutions on accident and force." The preference for "reflection and choice" over "accident and force" stands as a repudiation of Burkeanism.

Consider too the words of James Madison, writing in a very young America: "Is it not the glory of the people of America, that, whilst they have paid a decent regard to the opinions of former times and other nations, they have not suffered a blind veneration for antiquity, for custom, or for names, to overrule the suggestions of their own good sense, the knowledge of their own situation, and the lessons of their own experience?" In Madison's account, Americans "accomplished a revolution which has no parallel in the annals of human society. They reared the fabrics of governments which have no model on the face of the globe."[10]

These are largely rhetorical passages, but there is actually an argument in the background. Thomas Jefferson captured that argument with his lament that some people "ascribe to the men of the preceding age a wisdom more than human," and his response that the age of the founders "was very like the present, but without the experience of the present; and forty years of experience in government is worth a century of book-reading."[11] Jefferson is contending that current generations have more experience than past generations; in that sense, they have lived longer. Burkeans tend to cherish the wisdom of those long dead, but their stock of wisdom was far more limited than ours. In the same vein, Pascal contended that we are the ancients: "Those whom we call ancient were really new in all things, and properly constituted the infancy of mankind; and as we have joined to their knowledge the experience of the centuries which have followed them, it is in ourselves that we should find this antiquity that we revere in others."[12]

Jeremy Bentham attacked ancient wisdom in identical terms, contending that those who were ancient were, in the relevant sense, very young.[13] Bentham acknowledged that old people have more experience than young people, but insisted that "as between generation and generation, the reverse of this is true." In fact, "the wisdom of the times called old" is "the wisdom of the cradle." Bentham deplored the "reigning prejudice in favor of the dead," and also the tendency to disparage the present generation, which has a greater stock of knowledge than "untaught, inexperienced generations."

These arguments turn chronology directly against Burke, not by attempting to vindicate abstract reason, but by suggesting that if experience is our guide, the present has large advantages over the past. A similar idea might be found in the Court's suggestion, when invalidating a ban on same-sex sodomy, that what is crucial is not ancient practice, but "an emerging awareness that liberty gives substantial protection to adult persons in deciding how to conduct their private lives in matters pertaining to sex." And when the Court struck down bans on same-sex marriage, it emphasized "new insight" and how "we learn" the meaning of liberty.

But if their focus is on the Supreme Court, Burkean Minimalists do not have to insist that respect for longstanding traditions always makes sense in the political domain. Focusing on courts in particular, Burkean Minimalists might say that they are agnostic on the proper treatment of traditions in democratic processes. They might contend more modestly that their approach is for courts, because it is distinctly well adapted to the institutional strengths and weaknesses of the federal judiciary. For judges, the question is an insistently comparative one. It is not whether traditions are good, or great, in the abstract. It is whether tradition-tethered judges are better than judges who think that they ought to subject traditions to critical scrutiny. Burkean Minimalists insist that for fallible judges, traditions are the best available guide.

Decision Costs, Error Costs, and Minimalism

We should now be able to see the conditions under which Burkean minimalism makes most sense. Suppose, first, that originalism would produce intolerable results, in part because it would be too destabilizing. Suppose, second, that we have reason to distrust the theory-building capacities of judges, so that heroism is out of bounds. Suppose, finally, that in general or in particular areas, traditions and established practices are more reliable than the results that would be produced by those who are willing to subject those traditions and practices to critical scrutiny. When these conditions are met, the argument for Burkean minimalism has a lot of force.

As we have seen, no approach to the Constitution makes sense in all contexts or in every imaginable world. In our world, Burkean minimalism has clear advantages over originalism. It also has clear advantages over heroism of any kind insofar as there is reason to distrust the theory-building powers of federal judges, and to think that most of the time, longstanding practices are likely to make some sense, or at least enough so to stand against judicial scrutiny. Burkean minimalism has similar advantages over across-the-board soldiering, which is appealing in the abstract, but which would wreak havoc with traditions that have served the nation well.

The contest between Burkean minimalism and its rationalist sibling is much closer. Under some constitutional provisions, above all the equal protection clause, the Burkean approach is hard or even impossible to square with the most basic and entrenched understandings in American constitutional law. For that reason, it turns out to be self-contradictory: Burkeanism is inconsistent with traditions and self-defeating for that reason. The equal protection clause was self-consciously designed as an attack on longstanding practices; it reflects a principle that was not rooted in traditions at all.

Under that clause, a form of rationalism, allowing challenges to certain forms of discrimination, is part of the fabric of constitutional law, even if it requires occasional heroism. An even more serious problem is that for some forms of discrimination, it is exceedingly difficult to argue that longstanding traditions reflect wisdom, rather than power and injustice. Here the argument for a form of rationalism, subjecting traditions to critical scrutiny, is quite powerful. In this context, Burke's celebration of "prejudice" makes no sense.

For both free speech and religious liberty, the Court has embraced a form of rationalism, requiring traditions to be held to account. The result has often been minimalist, as in cases protecting commercial advertising, but it has sometimes been heroic, as in *New York Times v. Sullivan*, protecting free speech by imposing serious barriers to the use of libel law. My own view is that the Court should have been far more soldierly in the area of commercial advertising, because the free speech principle is above all focused on democratic self-government. I also believe that the Court should have been more minimalist in the context of libel law, where the Court's heroic approach has ignored the difficulty of the tradeoffs between free speech and preservation of people's reputations. But in both cases, a Burkean approach would be too cautious; it would have made our constitutional system worse, not better. In these areas, rationalist minimalism is preferable.

But in other domains, the Burkean approach can claim both to be consistent with existing law and to operate in a way that imposes the right kinds of discipline on judicial judgments. We have seen that in the areas of separation of powers and national security, Burkean minimalism has had a major role, as the Court has proceeded through small steps and with close attention to institutional practices extending over time. Justice Frankfurter offered the clearest statement of the Burkean position, with his suggestion that "a systematic, unbroken, executive practice, long pursued to the knowledge of the Congress and never before questioned, engaged in by Presidents who have also sworn to uphold the Constitution . . . may be treated as a gloss on 'executive Power' vested in the President."[14] In the particular context of national security, there are strong arguments against an aggressive or heroic judicial role in opposition to the elected branches, simply because this is a domain in which judicial expertise is unlikely.

I have emphasized that the argument for Burkean minimalism is stronger in some domains than in others. It is hardly an approach for all times and places. Often reasons should be required, and it is not enough to point to longstanding practices. But the central point is clear. Where originalism would produce unacceptable consequences, where traditions deserve respect, and where there is reason to distrust the theory-building capacities of federal judges, Burkean minimalism has a strong and enduring claim on our attention.

CHAPTER FOUR

Unanimity and Disagreement

As a matter of history, where do the Personae come from? Under what circumstances have individual justices felt free to state their own views?

These are closely linked questions. If the Court is largely unanimous, we will have fewer glimpses of the various Personae, and certainly fewer glimpses of the conflicts among them. As we will see, Heroes sometimes have trouble commanding a consensus within the Court, and Soldiers sometimes have real difficulty doing so. If the Court is unanimous, it will more likely be controlled by Minimalists. To have a larger perspective on the Personae and their sources, we have to investigate voting patterns within the Court—and some dramatic changes over time.

It is common to notice, and sometimes to deplore, the absence of consensus on the Supreme Court. On many of the great issues of the day, the Court has been divided 5–4, often with two or more of the Personae in intense disagreement. Explicitly concerned about the problem of legitimacy, and favorably disposed toward minimalism, Chief

Justice John Roberts suggested in 2006 that the Court should reorient itself in the direction of greater unanimity and fewer separate opinions.[1] Roberts contended that "the most successful chief justices help their colleagues speak with one voice." In his view, "Unanimous, or nearly unanimous, decisions are hard to overturn and contribute to the stability of the law and the continuity of the Court; by contrast, closely divided, 5–4 decisions make it harder for the public to respect the Court as an impartial institution that transcends partisan politics." As we have seen, many of the most intense disagreements pit Heroes against Soldiers.

In this chapter, I have three goals. The first is to offer an account of voting patterns within the Supreme Court over time. As we shall see, it is only a modest oversimplification to say that the Court has had two eras, divided by a single year: 1941. Before that year, the Court was overwhelmingly likely to decide cases without either dissents or separate concurrences, and 5–4 divisions were exceedingly rare. Between 1801 and 1940, the relevant patterns were essentially identical. After 1941, dissents and concurrences suddenly became routine, and 5–4 divisions became unremarkable. In important respects, the modern Supreme Court was born in 1941. The four Personae can certainly be found before that time—but there is no question that their full appearance required the post-1940 patterns.

Those remarkable patterns are known among political scientists, who initially established their existence,[2] but they are not widely appreciated. They should and can be, with the aid of statistical analysis. As we shall see, an understanding of the patterns has broad implications for thinking not only about the Supreme Court and Constitutional Personae but also about the role of institutional leaders, the emergence and revision of norms, and the conditions for multiple equilibria in law and politics.

My second goal is to explain those patterns, including the rise of the norm of consensus, the shift in 1941, and the relative stability of the post-1941 period. Was the pre-1941 period a kind of imposition, brought about by the force of tradition and the persuasiveness and authority of relevant chief justices, above all Chief Justice John Marshall? And what explains the sudden transformation—and the fact that it has proved robust? If we exercised our imaginations, we could envision a Court—in, say, 1970, or 1980, or 2015—that returned to the patterns of the pre-1941 era. The fact that to date, such a court belongs to the realm of the imagination requires a separate explanation.

My third goal is to evaluate the post-1940 status quo, in which we see frequent separate opinions, Personae in conflict, and a high rate of 5–4 decisions (on average, about 17 percent annually). Those who approve of the pre-1941 norm defend their view by reference to the values of institutional credibility, stability, and minimalism. As we shall see, however, their arguments depend on empirical assumptions that are unlikely to hold true. As we shall also see, a lot of people think that the breakdown in unanimity is a significant problem for both the Court and the nation as a whole. But at least in general, there is no good reason to accept that view. The Personae, emerging in full force from divided opinions, are not, on balance, a disservice to either the Court or the nation.

THE TRANSFORMATION OF 1941

For orientation, the three figures below show the rates of dissents, concurrences, and divisions by one-vote margin (5–4 or 4–3) from 1801 through 2013.[3] The essential picture is immediately clear. It is as if the United States has had two courts, operating in accordance with different norms. Something quite dramatic happened in the early 1940s, and in particular, 1941 marks the beginning of the transformation.

It is particularly puzzling that the breakdown of consensus occurred not during but in the aftermath of a period in Supreme Court history

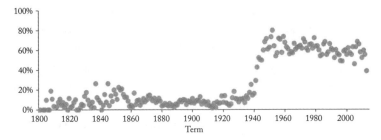

Figure 4.1 Percentage of Decisions with One or More Dissenting Opinions

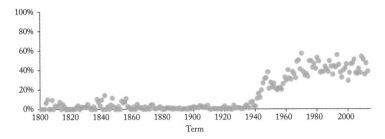

Figure 4.2 Percentage of Decisions with One or More Concurring Opinions

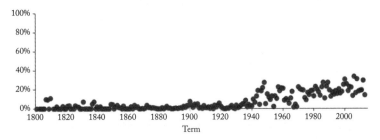

Figure 4.3 Percentage of Cases Decided by One Vote Margin

that is thought to be one of particular contestation, and that famously split the justices, often producing disagreements between Heroes and Soldiers. From 1905 until 1937, the Court was engaged in a series of intense contests with the executive branch, especially on constitutional questions involving the kinds of regulations associated with the New Deal and Progressive Eras. In some important cases, Heroes prevailed, as the Court struck down minimum wage and maximum hour legislation. The period between 1905 and 1937, often described as the *Lochner* era, was one in which a heroic Court invalidated a number of laws, and indeed, those years produced some of the most important, and most energetic, dissenting opinions in the Court's history. Many of those dissents came from Soldiers, above all Justice Holmes, objecting to constitutional heroism.

Notably, however, the norm of consensus was very much in force. In 1910, for example, 89 percent of the Court's decisions were unanimous, and between 1911 and 1935, the percentage of cases without any dissenting opinions was *always* over 80 percent. Whether Heroes prevailed, or Soldiers, or Minimalists, they were almost always able to speak for the Court as a whole.

In fact, 1937 is familiarly thought to be the year that the great debates between Heroes and Soldiers came to an end, with a famous retreat by the Court in the direction of soldiering in favor of President Roosevelt's New Deal. But between 1932 and 1937, when the conflict between the Roosevelt administration and the Court was at its height, the rate of unanimous decisions was quite high and saw a reduction only in 1937 itself, when significant doctrinal changes split the Court (see figure 4.4).

In 1937 and the years immediately following, Roosevelt was able to repopulate the Court with justices of his own choosing. In general, he hoped to appoint Soldiers, because a central goal was to immunize democratic judgments from judicial control. And in those years, the Court is not known for having been divided by historically important

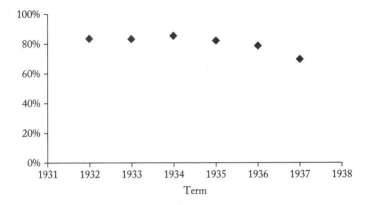

Figure 4.4 Percentage of Cases Decided Unanimously

disagreements. How puzzling, then, that consensus would break down within that repopulated Court and in a relatively quiet period.

To make progress on that puzzle, it is important to distinguish between an *actual consensus* on the one hand and a *norm of consensus* on the other. With an actual consensus, the justices truly agree with one another; they do not need any kind of norm to reach complete or near-unanimity. We might have nine Soldiers or nine Heroes, marching together. With a norm of consensus, by contrast, patterns of complete or near-unanimity will emerge even though the justices actually disagree. Soldiers and Heroes try to find common ground, or one group defers to the other. Because of the norm of consensus, the disagreement is not disclosed publicly, even if it is quite fundamental. In any period, it might be exceedingly difficult to know whether high levels of public agreement reflect actual consensus or a norm of consensus. As we will see, the historic patterns seem to have a great deal to do with a sudden decline of the norm of consensus, and much less with an increase in actual disagreement.

Of course I am speaking of aggregate cases, and not of particular disputes, where dissents can be found, and where disagreements were occasionally intense. The Court was famously divided in some of the great cases in American law, including *Dred Scott v. Sanford* (upholding the institution of slavery), *Lochner* itself (striking down maximum hour laws), *Whitney v. California* (allowing restrictions on free speech), and *Adkins v. Children's Hospital* (striking down minimum wage laws). In all of these cases, Soldiers and Heroes were in open conflict. In this light, we might describe the prevailing norm of consensus as suggesting that members of the Court *should not express disagreement unless they were justified in doing so in light of the intensity of their disagreement and the magnitude of the stakes.* As we shall see, this formulation seems to capture an understanding established under Chief Justice John Marshall.

EXPLANATIONS

What accounts for the observed patterns? In this section, I discuss, in sequence, the norm of consensus, the dramatic change in 1941, and the longstanding persistence of the patterns initially established in that year.

THE NORM OF CONSENSUS

A Little History

Among historians, it is well known that Chief Justice John Marshall worked exceedingly hard, and quite successfully, to produce a norm in favor of unanimity. Successful creation of that norm was hardly foreordained. With another chief justice, the Court might have taken a radically different course. (I am bracketing the question of Marshall's preferred Persona; in important cases, he was alternately Hero, Soldier, Minimalist, and Mute, but that's a story for another day.)

In its initial years under Chief Justice John Jay, the Court decided cases seriatim, with opinions published by reverse seniority, so that the chief justice delivered his opinion last. Often the last opinion was followed by a brief paragraph announcing the outcome, headed with three words: "By the Court."[4] Chief Justice Jay was succeeded by Oliver Ellsworth, who maintained a great deal of continuity with this practice, but who also reduced the tribunal's reliance on seriatim opinions and increased use of opinions of the Court, personally announced by the chief justice. We do not know if Ellsworth thought that it was important to make this shift, or whether it was a simple matter of convenience.

Apparently focusing on the need for institutional legitimacy and prestige—for creating a strong and nationally respected Supreme Court—Marshall went much further. He rejected the seriatim method of rendering decisions, and he worked successfully to promote unanimity within the Court. Under his leadership, the preexisting "By the Court" paragraph was transformed into the modern "Opinion of the Court." Marshall strongly discouraged dissents, and he himself wrote a large number of the Court's opinions, even if he was not in agreement with the ruling, thus fortifying the idea of public unanimity. Under Marshall's leadership, seriatim opinions disappeared. As Marshall explained, "The course of every tribunal must necessarily be, that the opinion which is delivered as the opinion of the court, is previously submitted to the judges; and, if any of the reasoning be disapproved, it must be so modified as to receive the approbation of all before it can be delivered as the opinion of all."[5]

Importantly, and oddly from the contemporary standpoint, the "Opinions of the Court" were ambiguous with respect to the question whether they reflected the views of all of the justices or only a majority. The public could not know the answer to that question; if a particular judge did not write separately, his own views would not be revealed. Because silence did not necessarily mean agreement, this practice reduced the pressure to write separately. It was clear that some justices, some of the time, silently acquiesced in the Court's rulings, and indeed, several published opinions explicitly acknowledged the norm in favor of acquiescence.

In one of his rare dissents, Marshall began with a disclaimer: "I should now, as is my custom, when I have the misfortune to differ from this Court, acquiesce silently in its opinion."[6] So did Joseph Story: "Had this been an ordinary case I should have contented myself with silence; but . . . I have thought it not unfit to pronounce my own opinion."[7] So did Bushrod Washington: "It has never been my habit to deliver dissenting opinions where it has been my misfortune to differ from those which have been pronounced by a majority of this Court."[8]

These statements reveal that some of the time, a norm of consensus was very much in force and accounted for the absence of a public dissent. Notwithstanding their silence, the justices did not actually agree. Because of his effectiveness in promoting that consensus, Marshall can be seen as a *norm entrepreneur*, one who was able to succeed in part because of his multiple skills and in part because of his distinctive role as chief justice. With respect to consensus and dissent, Marshall was undoubtedly the most important norm entrepreneur in the Court's history—with the possible exception of Harlan Fiske Stone, who was in crucial respects the anti-Marshall (as we shall see).

The practice of silent acquiescence was not without prominent critics. In a letter to his appointee William Johnson, Thomas Jefferson complained that with that practice, no one could possibly know "what opinion any individual member gave in any case, nor even that he who delivers the opinion, concurred in it himself." Jefferson objected that "the practice is certainly convenient for the lazy, the modest & the incompetent," because it "saves them the trouble of developing their opinion methodically and even of making up an opinion at all."[9]

In his illuminating response, Johnson explained that after his own appointment, a case arose "in which I differed from my brethren, and

I thought it a thing of course to deliver my opinion. But, during the rest of the session I heard nothing but lectures on the indecency of judges cutting at each other, and the loss of reputation which the Virginia appellate court had sustained by pursuing such a course. At length I found that I must either submit to circumstances or become such a cypher in our consultations as to effect no good at all."[10] Interestingly, and in a way that seemed to support Jefferson's emphasis on convenience "for the lazy, the modest & the incompetent," Johnson went on to suggest that the "real cause" of silent acquiescence was a desire to protect the justices who lacked either the will or the ability to write separately. For justices who lacked the capacity to explain their views, silent acquiescence had significant advantages, because it relieved them of the obligation to say what they thought.

Marshall served as chief justice for thirty-four years, and by the time he left the bench, the norm of consensus had become entrenched. For more than a century after his departure, the norm persisted. Until 1941, all of Marshall's successors appeared to favor it. For example, Chief Justice Chase said "that except in very important causes [filing] dissents [was] inexpedient."[11] Chief Justice Taft strongly believed in the maxim "no dissent unless absolutely necessary." He once explained: "I don't approve of dissents generally, for I think in many cases where I differ from the majority, it is more important to stand by the Court and give its judgment weight than merely to record my individual dissent where it is better to have the law certain than to have it settled either way."[12] He wrote to Stone personally, "I am quite anxious, as I am sure we are all, that the continuity and weight of our opinions on important questions of law should not be broken any more than we can help by dissents. . . . I hope you will look into the matter with care, because 5 to 4 decisions of the Court, while they must sometimes occur, don't help the weight of its judgment."[13] Chief Justice Hughes agreed with Taft. Justice Pierce Butler captured the longstanding view: "I shall in silence acquiesce. Dissents seldom aid in the right development or statement of the law. They often do harm. For myself I say: 'lead us not into temptation.'"[14]

Justice Holmes and Justice Brandeis—usually Soldiers, opposing the Court's anti-progressive Heroes—are sometimes treated as history's "great dissenters," but their behavior did not depart dramatically from the standards of the period, with an average of 2.48 and 4.4 dissents per term. These rates are strikingly low compared to, for example, the rates of 10.9 for Felix Frankfurter, 14.29 for William O. Douglas, 5.94 for William Brennan, and even 5.5 for Louis Powell, known as a centrist and hardly a dissenter.

It is clear that in 1941, the norm in favor of consensus collapsed, and with spectacular speed. What happened? There are many possible explanations; I focus here on the two most plausible.

Chief Justice Stone

In 1941, Harlan Fiske Stone was elevated to the position of Chief Justice. In the relevant respects, he was the anti-Marshall. Generally a Soldier (in voting to uphold economic regulation) but with unmistakable heroic inclinations (in emphasizing the importance of protecting democracy itself), Stone was insistent on the value of individual self-expression within the Court. In sharp contrast to his predecessors, Stone was uninterested in consensus, and he actually seemed to favor the transformation that occurred on his watch. He chafed under the control of Chief Justice Hughes and strenuously resisted the idea of silent acquiescence.

As early as 1930, Justice James McReynolds implored Stone not to dissent: "If the Court is broken down, then there will be rejoicing in certain quarters. I cannot think the last 3 dissents which you have sent me will aid you, the law or the Court." Stone's answer was revealing. He complained that if the majority "insists in putting our opinions which do not consider or deal with questions raised by the minority, it must, I think, be expected that the minority will give some expression to its views."[15]

As Stone wrote in a candid passage, unambiguously separating himself from Marshall and his successors, "The right of dissent is an important one and has proved to be such in the history of the Supreme Court. I do not think it is the appropriate function of a Chief Justice to attempt to dissuade members of the Court from dissenting in individual cases." Indeed, Stone linked dissent with the development of sound principles, which, he contended, "are the ultimate resultant of the abrasive force of the clash of competing and sometimes conflicting ideas."[16]

His own behavior tracked his stated conviction. As chief justice, he dissented 13.5 percent of the time, a far higher rate than that of any of his predecessors, and a higher rate than that of his two immediate successors as well (see table 4.1).

Chief Justice Stone did not merely welcome dissents and practice what he preached. He also helped initiated a large number of internal changes that were highly conducive to a breakdown of the previous norms.[17] These included significantly longer discussions in conference, in which competing positions were offered and debated, and in which separate coalitions were developed, often opposing Soldiers to Heroes. Under his leadership, the Court also abandoned its previous rule in favor of twenty-four-hour deadlines for commenting on drafts—thus allowing for more extensive responses, which could easily be developed into concurrences and dissents. With these changes, the Court began to develop into separate law offices, with individual justices elaborating their own views, and feeling far freer to express those views in public, thus ensuring numerous conflicts among the various Personae.

Table 4.1 Dissent Behavior of Eleven Chief Justices*

Chief Justice	Number of Cases	Number of Cases Justice Dissents	Dissent Proportion[a]
Marshall	1187	7	.0058
Taney	1708	38	.0222
Chase	1109	33	.0297
Waite	2642	45	.0170
Fuller	4866	113	.0232
White	2541	39	.0153
Taft	1708	16	.0093
Hughes	2050	46	.224
Stone	704	95	.1349
Vinson	723	90	.1244
Warren	1772	215	.1213

Source: Ulmer (1986), p. 53.
[a]Number of chief justice dissents divided by number of cases.

New and Independent-Minded Justices

On the basis of these points, it would be possible to conclude that
with respect to the transformation of 1941, "Chief Justice Stone did
it." But the conclusion is too simple. In the relevant period, the Court
experienced extraordinarily rapid turnover. Roosevelt appointed Hugo
Black in 1937, followed by Stanley Reed in 1938, Felix Frankfurter and
William O. Douglas in 1939, Frank Murphy in 1940, and James Byrnes
and Robert Jackson in 1941, when Stone became chief justice. Between
1937 and 1941, the Court was a radically transformed tribunal, with only
one holdover member in addition to Stone (Owen Roberts, appointed
in 1930). As I have noted, the transformation deepens the puzzle. It
might not have been anticipated that there would be a sudden outbreak
of concurrences and dissents with effectively eight Roosevelt selec-
tions sitting with Justice Roberts. Appointment by the same president
should dampen disagreement, or so it might be thought. Roosevelt

wanted Soldiers, and if the Court consisted solely of them, we would anticipate a lot of unanimity. Justices with similar views might not be expected to reject a norm of consensus, and they might be expected to agree in fact, whatever the prevailing norm with respect to public expression of disagreement.

Indeed, it might well be questioned whether and when a chief justice is either a necessary or sufficient condition for the transformation. If a norm in favor of consensus is well entrenched, and if most of the justices are acculturated and committed to it, it might be doubted whether a new chief justice could significantly alter it. If, for example, Stone had been chief justice in 1891, 1901, 1911, 1921, or 1931, a large-scale shift would probably not have occurred. The other members of the Court might well have resisted any effort to inaugurate such a shift. And if Hughes had been chief justice in 1941, it is worth wondering whether he would have been able to prevent at least some kind of change.

In this light, we might consider another hypothesis, which is that the new justices were uninterested in maintaining the old norm, and hence that any chief justice would have had real difficulty in doing so. On a strong version of the "new justices" hypothesis, Chief Justice Stone was neither necessary nor sufficient for the shift. On the weak version of the same hypothesis, Chief Justice Stone was necessary, but he was not sufficient.

The key point here is that the new justices, above all Frankfurter, favored a more academic atmosphere, in which justices would develop competing views and ultimately feel free to express them. Frankfurter was a Minimalist by nature, and often played the Soldier, but the central point is that he believed that the justices should express their own views. Consider Frankfurter's remarkable words, circulated to one of his colleagues: "Just because we agree in the result ... and because no immediately important public issue is involved by our different approaches in reaching the same legal result, it is at once interesting and profitable to discuss the underlying jurisprudential problem. And so I venture to make some observations on your opinion, I hope in the same spirit and for the same academic purpose as I would were I writing a piece as a professor in the *Harvard Law Review*."[18] In a Memorandum for the Conference, Frankfurter wrote that while "unanimity is an appealing abstraction," it is also true that "a single Court statement on important constitutional issues and other aspects of public law is bound to smother differences that in the interests of candor and of the best interest of the Court ought to be express."[19] He did not quite justify that conclusion—why, exactly, is it bad "to smother differences"?—but his own preferences were clear.

In terms of his desire for self-expression, Frankfurter was an extreme case, certainly in the early 1940s, but Douglas had been a professor as well, and as the course of his career demonstrates, he was fully willing to speak on his own (eventually becoming a leading Hero, especially for the protection of civil liberties). Hugo Black was not so different (and a civil liberties Hero as well), and Jackson of course had a unique voice, which he was hardly averse to using. Frankfurter, Douglas, Black, and Jackson also had strong personalities, and as recent members of the Court, they had not been fully socialized into a judicial culture that prized a norm of consensus. Because of their relative youth and inexperience, we might wonder whether they were likely to accept that norm lightly. At least once Stone essentially unleashed them, they were likely to break the norm down. We cannot say whether and to what extent they would have done so without Stone, or whether and to what extent a more directive chief justice, intent on preserving the longstanding norm, might have been able to succeed. But we might want to conclude that the combination was a perfect storm.

This is a tempting conclusion, but it does run into serious empirical objection.[20] From 1937 to 1940, a number of the new justices sat on the Court, but they did not show significant levels of independent

Table 4.2 Dissent Rates of Associate Justices, before and after Stone Became Chief Justice

Justice	Pre-Stone Terms Dissent Rates (%)				Stone Terms Dissent Rates (%)	
	1937	1938	1939	1940	1941	1942
Black	5.26	4.32	1.46	2.42	6.62	8.16
Reed		1.44	0.73	1.21	3.97	2.72
Frankfurter			0	1.21	3.97	8.16
Douglas			0.73	0.61	0.66	0.68
Murphy				0	0	6.8

Sources: Thomas Walker et al., *On the Mysterious Demise of Consensual Norm in the United States Supreme Court*, 50 J POLITICS 361 (1988), Table 4; EPSTEIN ET AL., THE SUPREME COURT COMPENDIUM: DATA, DECISIONS, AND DEVELOPMENTS, 5th ed. (2012).

opinion-writing. Consider table 4.2, which shows the percentage of cases each term in which a justice wrote a dissenting opinion, using the opinions of the new justices from 1937 to 1942.

Black, Douglas, and Frankfurter eventually turned out to be especially frequent dissenters, with the heroism of the first two often opposing the soldiering of the third; but their propensity to write separately did not emerge until Stone became chief justice. The same is true of Reed and Murphy. From the data, it does appear that Stone was a necessary condition for these and other justices to write separately. We cannot exclude the possibility that eventually, they would have started to do so. But with this evidence, it seems that a dissent-friendly chief justice—a norm entrepreneur in his own way—might well have been an essential condition for the transformation that took place in 1941. The strong version of the "new justices" hypothesis does not fit the facts, but we cannot exclude the possibility that the weak version is correct.

WHY HAVE THE PATTERNS BEEN RELATIVELY
STABLE AFTER 1941?

How do we explain the relative consistency of the relevant patterns over more than six decades? It should be clear that for those patterns to persist, two conditions are necessary. First, the level of actual disagreement must remain relatively constant. Second, the norms that govern the expression of disagreement must remain relatively constant as well. Let us begin with actual disagreement.

Actual Disagreement

A potential explanation is that both Democratic and Republican presidents appoint justices, and unless one party dominates the presidency for a sustained period, the Court will be predictably divided between Democratic and Republican appointees—hence a significant amount of division, resulting in dissents, concurrences, and 5–4 splits. This explanation is especially tempting if we restrict ourselves to the period from 2009, when the Court included five justices appointed by Republican presidents and four appointed by Democrats. Of course it is true that Republican heroism often opposes Democratic soldiering (on, for example, campaign finance, gun control, commercial advertising, and affirmative action), while Republican soldiering often opposes Democratic heroism (on, for example, abortion rights, sex discrimination, the rights of criminal defendants, and issues involving sexual orientation).

The difficulty with this explanation is that surprisingly, comparable levels of disagreement can be found regardless of whether the Court has consisted of a nearly even division of Democratic and Republican appointees, or whether it has consisted largely of appointees from presidents of a single political party. As we have seen, the modern patterns were born in a period in which the Court was dominated by Democratic appointees. And from the period 1981–2015, the Court was generally dominated by Republican appointees. In 1981, the Court had two Democratic appointees (Thurgood Marshall and Byron White) and seven Republicans (William Brennan, Harry Blackmun, John Paul Stevens, Warren Burger, Lewis Powell, Sandra Day O'Connor, and John Paul Stevens). In 2001, there was a similar 7–2 split in favor of Republican appointees. The percentage of 5–4 splits cannot be shown to have declined when presidents of a single party have been able to select a large majority of the Court's members.

A different explanation is that since the 1940s, the Court has often been evenly divided on ideological grounds, in part because Republican presidents have made some liberal or moderate choices (whether intentionally or by mistake). There is no question that William Brennan (an Eisenhower appointee) and Harry Blackmun (a Nixon appointee) showed quite liberal voting patterns. Many Republicans were disappointed by Stevens (a Ford appointee) and David Souter (appointed by George H. W. Bush). Perhaps the relative consistency of internal divisions is a product of persistent ideological splits within the Court.

There is something to this explanation, but it is not adequate. To see why, consider a thought experiment. Let us imagine that over the next decade, the Court shifts significantly to the right. Suppose that the only two retirements come from Justices Breyer and Ginsburg, and that they are replaced by people who tend to agree with Justices Scalia and Thomas. In that event, the Court's center of gravity would shift dramatically, with an apparent "bloc" of six conservatives (Scalia, Thomas, Roberts, Alito, and the two new members). Should we expect to see a sharp reduction in internal divisions?

The answer is not necessarily, and for one reason: Lawyers and lower-court judges are highly alert to the composition of the Court. If the Court shifts in any particular direction, we will almost certainly see a very different set of rulings in the lower courts, whose judges are most unlikely to issue decisions that are overwhelmingly likely to be reversed. The central point is that the cases that the Court hears will consist, in large part, of issues that are difficult not in the abstract, but *in light of the Court's particular composition at the time*. It follows that in the modern era, a significant level of (actual) internal disagreement is highly likely to persist, and that unless the justices adopt a norm in favor of consensus, any Supreme Court will probably seem divided in a significant number of important cases. The reason is that in a hierarchical legal system, the Court will end up hearing disputes that are likely to split its current members—and this is true even if their approach to the law, or their ideology, changes radically over time. Whatever the Court's composition, we will see Heroes, Soldiers, Minimalists, and Mutes, if only because the nature of the cases that the Court hears will shift along with its composition.

Expressed Disagreement

Why has the norm itself remained relatively stable since 1941? Have different kinds of people been appointed to the Court? Are they more strong-willed and independent? Do we have more self-conscious Heroes and more self-conscious Soldiers? More Minimalists? Affirmative answers cannot be ruled out. A full account might well have to distinguish among periods; the persistence of the norm in the 1980s might not have the same explanation as the persistence of that norm in the 1990s or 2000s.

To investigate such questions, a detailed historical account might well be necessary. But the simple and most general answer is that the justices have not had a sufficient motivation to alter it. The question is what individual justices prefer. Whether they are Heroes, Soldiers, Minimalists, or Mutes, they appear to want to say what they think. (Mutes of course prefer silence, but sometimes they have to explain that particular preference.) From their standpoint, the costs of returning to the pre-1941 norm would apparently be high, because the result would be a significant degree of self-silencing. Of course those costs might be worth incurring if the justices did not want to expend the effort that is necessary to write separately. Recall that on one account, the early triumph of the norm on the Marshall Court had something to do with a desire not to expend that effort. But there is no reason to think that members of the current Court, or their successors, will want to promote a consensus norm.

It is certainly imaginable that a chief justice could produce some movement in the direction of that norm. We lack direct evidence that any chief justice has tried, in any serious or systematic way, to restore such a norm, and in any case there is reason to wonder whether any such effort would be likely to succeed. For more than seventy years, justices have generally felt free to express their views, and any norm in favor of self-silencing appears to have been weak (though we cannot exclude the possibility that it exists in some moderate form). With a longstanding tradition in favor of expressing independent view, a chief justice would have to be both ambitious and exceedingly skillful if he sought to move toward the pre-1941 norm. As noted, Chief Justice Roberts is on record as favoring a reduction in separate opinions and an increase in unanimity; in general, however, he has not been able to produce real change.

EVALUATING THE MODERN ERA

Expressed disagreement will have both benefits and costs. From the standpoint of the individual justice, the calculation may be very different from what it is from the standpoint of society as a whole. To understand the judgments of individual justices, we need to know what they maximize. Some justices care greatly about their personal legacy, and if they do, they will be more likely to stake out their own ground (and to favor and promote a norm in favor of separate statements). If they are strongly committed, in particular areas, to heroism or soldiering, they will want to make their views norm. Justices also care about the development of the law as such. My analysis here focuses principally on what is best for society as a whole, rather than on the calculus for individual justices.

Let us start with benefits, signaled by Jefferson's early complaint and captured briefly in Justice William Brennan's suggestion: "Through dynamic interaction among members of the present Court and through dialogue across time with the future Court, we ensure the continuing contemporary relevance and hence vitality of the principles of our fundamental charter."[21]

THE BENEFITS OF DISAGREEMENT

The principal benefits of expressed disagreement fall into four categories.

Future Adjudication

A dissent (or a separate concurrence) might have desirable effects on the future development of the law. If a justice supports soldiering, and if he loses to a heroic majority, he might want to put some kind of stake in the ground, and he might want everyone to see it. Perhaps justices will eventually find his view to be persuasive; it might provide a kind of lodestar for posterity. Indeed, numerous dissents have become the law of the land. Insofar as they generally favored soldiering in the economic realm, Justices Holmes and Brandeis did end up persuading their successors. And insofar as they argued for a strong right to freedom of speech—and to that extent assumed the role of the Hero—they have also been vindicated by history. In many cases, dissenters undoubtedly hope that their views will end up producing a corrective.

To evaluate this possibility in a disciplined way, it is necessary to focus on two factors: the likelihood that a dissent will have that effect and the value of the effect if it should occur. If the real goal is to alter the course of the law—to produce more soldiering, more heroism, more minimalism—it might not be worthwhile to produce a dissent if the chance of alteration is zero. But even if the chance is relatively low, it might be worth writing separately if the value of a change is extremely high. These simple points help to explain the intuitive point that in cases of great importance, where a justice believes that the Court has made a damaging and harmful mistake, the incentive to dissent is increased. Even in the pre-1941 era, justices appear to have produced dissents in part for this reason. From the social point of view, a dissent has an "expected value" in terms of effects on future justices, and in some cases, the expected value might be high.

We should distinguish here between two kinds of effects on future adjudication. In the most dramatic cases, the Court's opinion is actually overruled. In less dramatic cases, the Court's opinion is read narrowly, or at least not expanded. A powerful dissent might be worthwhile if it has the latter consequence. Indeed, a dissent might be written specifically to have that consequence. Here as well, there is an expected value in terms of benefits, and it might be high.

Congress

Even if a dissent is not likely to move a future Court, it might influence Congress. If a justice signals that the Court has erred and that the stakes are high, she might trigger legislative attention. Here again, a prospective dissenter would do well to consider both the probability that a dissent will have that effect and the value of the effect if it should occur. In the abstract, it is reasonable to think that for legislators, results are what matter, and not dissenting opinions, and that dissents will, at most, create a modest increase in the incentive to correct what legislators would already see as a mistake or an injustice. Pointing to that increase, heroic justices are particularly inclined to favor dissents for this reason. Perhaps a majority of the Court could not be persuaded to invalidate legislation, but perhaps Congress could be persuaded to fix it.

Justices who believe that separate opinions will have large effects on Congress might be suffering from optimistic bias (the human propensity to be more optimistic than reality warrants) or the spotlight effect (which makes people think, wrongly, that other people are looking at them, as if they are under some kind of spotlight). But even if a dissenting opinion increases the likelihood of a legislative response only modestly, it might be worthwhile to write it.

The Chastened (and Wiser) Majority?

Even if a dissent has no influence on future justices or Congress, it might improve the majority opinion, perhaps by convincing the justices in the majority to scale back their opinion or to move it in somewhat different directions. A judge who favors minimalism might be able to persuade would-be Heroes to restrain themselves. A judge who favors soldiering might be able to persuade Minimalists to shift their opinion a bit more in the direction of respect for the democratic process.

Of course it is true that having done that work, the author of a dissenting opinion might choose not to publish what she writes—but the effects of a dissent might well depend on a credible commitment to publish. We lack systematic evidence with respect to the claim that dissenting opinions improve or even materially alter opinions of the Court. For obvious reasons, such evidence would be exceedingly difficult to compile. But it is more than plausible to think that both the possibility and the actuality of dissenting opinions have a beneficial effect on the Court's majorities.

Educating the Public

The Court's opinions can have an educative function. If the justices disagree, and state their disagreement publicly, people can have a sense of the competing views, and can understand the issues a bit better. Maybe the public can see why soldiering or minimalism have real appeal—or why heroism poses real risks. A single opinion, in which the Court speaks as one, may do far less to promote understanding. Of course it is possible to ask why, exactly, an improved understanding is better. But perhaps it is desirable for the public to have a sense of why people disagree on legal issues. An understanding of the nature and sources of disagreement may have both short-term and long-term effects in spurring people to attend to important problems.

Those who object to internal division are likely to contend that these various benefits are overstated. But their principal concern, traceable to Marshall's era, involves the costs of division. Like the benefits, the costs appear to fall into three different categories.

CREDIBILITY, LEGITIMACY, AND "MONOLITHIC SOLIDARITY"

In calling for a "refocus on functioning as an institution," Chief Justice Roberts said that with its post-1941 patterns, the Court risked a loss of "its credibility and legitimacy." As he saw it, internal divisions could threaten the Court's image in the eyes of the public. Learned Hand saw things similarly, writing that a dissenting opinion "cancels the impact of monolithic solidarity on which the authority of a bench of judges so largely depends."[22] For example, a heroic opinion might lose its authority if four members of the Court disagree with it.

Hypotheses

Whenever the Court is not unanimous, we might speculate that its credibility is at risk, because a competing view will be offered, and it might be expressed vigorously. *Brown v. Board of Education* was famously unanimous, and Chief Justice Warren worked exceedingly hard to ensure that the nation would see that the justices were in total agreement. In his view, a divided Court would sacrifice its legitimacy in an area where legitimacy was crucial.

One reason is that the Court's decision was heroic, and certainly not soldierly. If the justices were taking on the institution of segregation and risking the enmity of a large portion of the nation, perhaps it was important that none of the justices played the role of the Soldier. And it is hardly implausible to think that from the standpoint of legitimacy, 5–4 divisions are especially troubling, because they suggest that with a change of a single vote, fundamental issues might have been resolved differently. The problem might well be aggravated if the division occurs along predictable political lines. *Bush v. Gore* is perhaps the most extreme example—on this count, the anti-*Brown*—because the Court's majority consisted solely of Republican appointees, and because the ultimate result was widely seen as highly politicized.

This concern is actually a hypothesis, to the effect that internal divisions weaken credibility. The hypothesis raises empirical questions: Are 5–4 decisions genuinely less credible than unanimous decisions, and if so, to what extent? Are 5–4 decisions less credible than 7–2 decisions, or than 8–1 decisions? In principle, those questions should be answerable. *Brown* was indeed unanimous, but its unanimity did not come close to quelling public opposition; for a long period, the Court's discussion sharply split the nation. Perhaps the opposition would have been even worse if the Court had been divided—but perhaps not.

Consider a competing hypothesis: *The credibility of Supreme Court decisions does not turn on the extent of the division within the Court, but instead on the relationship between those decisions and the prior convictions of relevant members of the public.* Under this hypothesis, everything depends on whether the Court's decision is consistent with people's prior convictions. If the Court ruled, in a bizarre fit of soldiering, that the Constitution gives the Environmental Protection Agency the power to arrest and imprison people at its whim, the public would be most unlikely to find the decisions credible and legitimate, even if the Court turned out to be unanimous. If, by contrast, the Court issued a ruling that is broadly acceptable, and that fits with widespread convictions, the public will not be much exercised whether its ruling is 9–0 or 5–4. And if the public is itself divided, the credibility of the Court's decision will depend on the relationship between those divisions and that decision. If the Court rules in favor of gun control, those who support gun control will find the decision credible, and those who reject gun control will not. On this view, people's prior convictions are what matter, not vote-counting.

Existing evidence remains sparse, but it tends to support this hypothesis. Larger majorities and unanimity do not seem to increase public acceptance of the Court's decisions. A 2009 study explored people's reaction to the controversial decision in *Kelo v. City of New London*, where the Court's majority, in a soldierly opinion, allowed the government to take private property for redistributive purposes.[23] Though the government paid the property owner for the taking, the decision was highly controversial, and many people (especially on the right) strenuously objected to it. In the relevant study, the presentation of the case was manipulated to change the size of the majority (which was actually 5–4). The results showed that the level of internal consensus had little effect on people's views. In terms of people's reactions, the Court's decision mattered, not the number of justices who supported it.

In a later study, it was found that "reaction to judicial consensus is dependent on the ideological salience of the issue involved" and that "the public is unmoved by the majority size in highly salient decisions."[24]

It is only in "cases with low salience," in the sense that people do not really know about them, that large majorities have an effect on public attitudes. When the issue is obscure, the level of internal disagreement matters, because people take unanimity as a signal that the case has a clear answer. But when the issue is well known, and when people have strong convictions about it, they are perfectly prepared to believe that a unanimous or near-unanimous court is wrong. If you despise a Supreme Court decision because it offends your deepest values, you are unlikely to be much moved by learning that all of the justices disagree with you.

The distinction between "high salience" and "low salience" has a close connection to the question whether people have clear anteced-ent convictions. When a case is highly salient, it is because it raises issues that trigger strong concerns (such as abortion, or freedom from surveillance, or discrimination on the basis of disability). When it has low salience, it is usually because it does not much matter to people, and hence their antecedent convictions are weak; they do not know what they think.

To say this is not to insist that even for highly salient cases, internal divisions cannot matter at all to the public's reaction. The existing evi-dence does not exclude the possibility that a unanimous decision can increase the Court's legitimacy and reduce concerns about politiciza-tion within the judiciary. Some people might well seize on any kind of dissent to show that their disagreement with the Court is reasonable, and a 5–4 decision (with a predictable division along ideological lines) might seem, to some citizens, less convincing than a unanimous or lopsided vote. Certainly a dissenting opinion can serve as a rhetorical resource for those who object to a decision. If the Court is being heroic, a Soldier's dissent might help inflame the public.

In the future, we should be able to obtain more evidence on the question whether 5–4 decisions are, in fact, less credible than other kinds of decisions. To be sure, we do not have randomized controlled trials, enabling us to explore whether, for example, cases involving gun rights, campaign finance restrictions, and abortion would have been less controversial if the Court had been undivided or less divided. But an experimental design could easily explore the question whether the public would receive these decisions, or related ones, differently with larger majorities. At the present time, the idea that 5–4 decisions pose a serious problem of credibility or legitimacy remains an unproven hypothesis.

How Important Is Credibility?

Suppose that a 5–4 decision is, in fact, less credible, and less likely to be perceived as legitimate, than a 9–0 decision. Does that fact suggest that justices should decline to express their doubts and join an opinion that they believe to be wrong? The answer is far from obvious.

On the one side is the cost of self-silencing: failing to provide the public with information that could inform its judgment about the underlying issues, and perhaps affect legislation, while also failing to provide posterity, including other justices, with that information as well. On the other side is the benefit: insulating the Court from criticism that it would otherwise receive. But how much of a benefit is that? Such insulation might well be unwarranted because there is, by hypothesis, internal disagreement on the Court. Maybe a heroic dissenter has a strong argument against a soldierly majority. Maybe the Court is upholding an action that really is invading individual rights, properly understood. Is it appropriate to insulate the Court from criticism, and from a challenge to its credibility, that would come from exposing that disagreement to public view? The answer is by no means clear.

We might want to make a distinction between a new court, initially struggling to establish its legitimacy, and a court whose essential legitimacy is clear and not truly contested. For the former court, there might well be an argument for reducing the appearance of internal contestation. The same might also be said of an established court that is resolving a highly contested question. As noted, *Brown v. Board of Education* is the most famous example, and as also noted, many people lamented the 5–4 division in *Bush v. Gore*, contending that the split vote suggested a high degree of politicization on questions of constitutional law. In some cases, unanimity might reduce that concern. But in general, we lack evidence to justify the belief that the post-1940 patterns have raised serious questions about the Court's legitimacy and credibility.

STABILITY AND CERTAINTY

Stability in judge-made law can be important, in part because those affected by law can benefit from a high degree of certainty. On this view, the problem with divided rulings is that they are *fragile*. It might be urged that the pre-1941 situation was better precisely because the Court's rulings were more fixed and firm. Note that this objection turns into a vice what supporters of dissenting opinions see as a virtue: the possibility that a dissenting opinion will eventually move the law.

This concern can take three different forms. The first is that when the Supreme Court is divided, its decisions are more likely to be overruled. The second is that when the Court is divided, its decisions are more likely to be cabined in the future—perhaps limited to their facts, and hence the law is more likely to take a meandering and unpredictable path. On this view, split rules will ensure a kind of case-by-case minimalism, not necessarily when they are issued, but as subsequent courts work to narrow them. The third concern is that litigants and lower courts are less likely to know what the law is and they are therefore more likely to be confused. All of these concerns raise empirical questions.

Overruling?

With respect to the first, we have some quantitative evidence, and it does provide some support for the claim that when the Court is sharply divided, its decisions are more fragile.[25] One study, analyzing data from 1946–95, finds that a precedent is more likely to be overruled if it is the product of a one-vote margin decision; a precedent is less likely to be overruled if its decision coalition was unanimous; and the larger the number of concurring opinions published with a precedent, the greater the chance it will be overruled.[26] More specifically, a minimum winning coalition (5–4) increases the risk of overruling by 53.6 percent, and a unanimous coalition decreases the risk of overruling by 46.9 percent. For each additional concurrence, the risk of the case being overruled increases by 22.4 percent.

These are large differences, but percentages should be taken with many grains of salt. The Court overrules very few of its decisions, and hence the risk that any particular decision will be overruled is exceedingly low. Even if the risk increased by 50 percent or more, it is still exceedingly unlikely to be overruled. More specifically, the Court has, in its history, overruled 1.2 percent of its decisions, and 1.7 percent of its 5–4 decisions. From the social standpoint, how meaningful is the relevant increase in probability? We do not even know that the 5–4 division causes the increase. It may be that 5–4 splits reflect the importance and difficulty of the underlying questions, and hence that cases that pose such questions would be more likely to be overruled even if they were unanimous.

To evaluate this evidence, moreover, we would have to distinguish between 9–0 decisions that reflect actual agreement and 9–0 decisions that reflect silent acquiescence. A norm of consensus means that dissenting justices will generally join the majority, notwithstanding their private views, and do not express those views in public. But they are nonetheless dissenters. An apparent 9–0 decision may be, in reality, a 5–4 split. Would the justices be less likely to overrule a secret 5–4 decision than a publicly expressed 5–4 decision? Maybe so, but the existing evidence does not enable us to answer that question.

Cabining?

It is certainly possible that when the Court is sharply divided, the Court itself, or lower courts, is more likely to read its opinion narrowly. Consider, for example, *Bush v. Gore*, which has not produced a set of new equal protection cases or spawned doctrinal departures—perhaps in part because of the internal division. From the minimalist standpoint, that's fine. But if we prize predictability, and disapprove of a situation in which constitutional law moves in fits and starts, with decisions that are limited to their facts, we might be especially concerned about the effects of internal division. Those who believe in the rule of law will not be excited about internal divisions if they make it hard for people to know what the law is.

Here as well, however, we need to begin by asking whether a norm of consensus is relevant: Are decisions that hide secret divisions, in which justices do not reveal their actual disagreement, less likely to be cabined than decisions with publicly expressed divisions? Perhaps lower courts and litigants care about what is expressed, because that is all that they see—a point that may argue for an increase in expressed unanimity. But within the Court itself, a division is a division, whether or not it is revealed to the public. For obvious reasons, it is not easy to study the question whether the justices are likely to read a decision narrowly if the justices are divided but do not disclose that fact.

In terms of how the Court reads its own decisions, two questions would seem to be central. The first is whether members of a majority—whether it is 5–4, 7–2, or 9–0—are ambivalent about the reasoning and the result. The number of justices who join the opinion may tell us very little about that question. Suppose that the justices are divided 5–4, but the members of the majority have issued a broad, declarative statement in which they have full confidence. If so, the five justices who constitute the majority might well proceed unimpeded. So long as they remain on the Court, there is not much reason to think that the ruling will be read narrowly. The second question is whether the composition of the Court changes over time. Changes in the Court's composition can of course lead to significant shifts in the law.

It is true that if one member of a 5–4 majority reads the decision very narrowly, and joined it on that understanding, a degree of cabining is highly likely. A single Minimalist might be able to constrain four would-be Heroes. But would things really be different if the four dissenters declined to express their views and thus made for a unanimous majority? It might be expected that with a norm of consensus, we would have to distinguish between real 9–0 decisions and 9–0 decisions that reflect silent acquiescence. Apparent 9–0 decisions, which are in fact 5–4 decisions, should produce the same future path as 5–4 divisions that are publicly disclosed as such.

Suppose it is true that when the Court is publicly divided 5–4, or when dissents are common, precedents are read more narrowly. Is that a problem? Minimalists favor unanimous opinions precisely *because* they produce greater narrowness. Whether narrowness is a problem, or instead a kind of solution, depends on the context.

Uncertainty?

Does a divided Supreme Court increase uncertainty? Does it make it harder for people to know what the law is? We can imagine extreme cases in which the answer is obvious. Suppose that in an issue involving freedom of speech or privacy, two justices write as Minimalists, four as Heroes, and three as Soldiers. If there is no majority opinion, and if a number of different justices write separately, it might be exceedingly difficult to know the content of the law. That is a genuine problem. The law cannot be certain if there is no opinion for the Court. But is there also uncertainty in the presence of some number of concurrences and dissents, or with a 5–4 division?

Again, the answer is by no means clear. We can easily imagine a 9–0 decision that leaves a lot of uncertainty, perhaps because it is vague and ambiguous, or perhaps because it is narrow and limited to the particular facts. A minimalist, 9–0 decision that provides no clear rule would seem to leave the law up for grabs. By contrast, a 5–4 decision might establish a clear, firm rule, one that everyone understands. Heroic decisions can be really clear, and the same is true for soldierly ones. If, for example, the Court ruled that the Constitution does not protect commercial advertising, the law would not be ambiguous, and people would have no need to guess. With respect to certainty, the most important question is the nature of the opinion and the judgment, not the number of justices who sign it.

How Important Is Stability?

Stability and certainty are important, to be sure, but their importance differs across areas. They are not always trump cards. Of course some areas of law need to be settled, so that people can organize their lives, and clear decisions might be best even if they are not ideal as a matter of principle. A specified speed limit (say, 65 miles per hour) is better than a vague one ("drive at reasonable speeds") even if the specified number is not precisely right. But if Supreme Court rulings are badly wrong and do significant damage, there is a strong argument in favor of destabilizing them. Indeed, a 5–4 division may itself be evidence that a decision deserves continuing scrutiny.

In sum, the argument from stability and certainty—if cast as an argument against internal divisions within the Court—rests on weak foundations. If we care about those very goals, apparent unanimity, which disguises internal divisions, is not much better than a 5–4 ruling. In any case, the goals are themselves an ingredient in the overall analysis, and not always decisive.

MINIMALISM

Suppose that justices embrace minimalism. If so, they might well be skeptical of divided courts and approve of a norm that encourages the justices to find a rationale on which all can agree. A norm in favor of unanimity will tend to produce minimalism, including both narrowness and shallowness. Chief Justice Roberts has pressed this particular point, urging that the "broader the agreement among the justices, the more likely it is a decision on the narrowest possible grounds."[27]

To see his point, imagine that the Supreme Court were currently governed by an unambiguous norm in favor of consensus. Such a norm might well incline the majority in the direction of taking on the concerns of the skeptics, producing narrow, shallow opinions. Heroes will have a hard time making common cause with Soldiers, but if the decision is minimalist, perhaps they can find some way to join together. We can imagine, for example, a minimalist opinion protecting a commercial advertisement under the First Amendment, while allowing heroic and soldierly justices to press their competing views about commercial advertising in the future.

Chief Justice Roberts's claim is that if a norm in favor of unanimity moved the Court in the direction of broad or universal agreement—and if potential dissenters had something akin to a veto power—minimalism would become far more likely. Instead of creating a broad right to choose abortion, for example, a norm of consensus might have led the Court to a minimalist ruling, striking down some state laws as unacceptable insofar as they prohibited abortion in cases of rape and incest. And indeed, the logic of Chief Justice Roberts's view is that he would approve of the direction toward greater narrowness and shallowness.

It follows that for those who favor minimalism, there is a plausible argument in favor of a norm of consensus. But even on its own terms, the argument is not airtight. If a norm of consensus is in play, the question is whether the majority must accommodate the views of the minority, or whether the minority must instead surrender to the majority. By itself, the norm of consensus is silent on that question. If the norm encourages the minority to surrender, then broad, deep rulings (and perhaps heroic ones) can be expected even from unanimous courts—an outcome that is, from the standpoint of minimalism, actually perverse.

The deeper problem—pressed by Heroes and Soldiers in particular—is that minimalism should not always be favored. We have seen the core of the argument in chapter 3; the central point is that the argument on behalf of minimalism depends largely on the costs of decisions and the costs of errors. In some cases, narrowness is a vice rather than a virtue, because it leaves uncertainty and unpredictability, and because a wider ruling would reduce both without introducing error. In some cases, depth is desirable, because it gives a clear sense of the grounds for the outcome, and offers a sound basis for future development. Minimalism is not an approach for all times and seasons. It follows that even if a norm of consensus would press the Court in the direction of minimalism, it is not clear that the norm is desirable.

A VERY BRIEF ACCOUNTING

It is tempting to lament the post-1941 period and to suggest that the old norm of consensus promoted the Court's credibility and legitimacy, helped stabilize the law, and increased the likelihood of minimalist rulings. No one should deny that if the Court is persistently fragmented, and if the fragmentation occurs along political grounds, some people will lose faith in it—especially if their preferred views are consistently rejected. In any particular historical period, an analysis of the costs and benefits of internal division may argue for an increase in self-silencing.

We have seen, however, that the arguments in favor of higher levels of consensus rest on fragile foundations. The post-1941 norm cannot be shown to compromise the Court's role in American government, or to disserve the constitutional order.

Closing Words

Rules of Attraction

HEROES, SOLDIERS, MINIMALISTS, and Mutes are the dominant figures in American constitutional law. They appear in every era, and as long as there is a Supreme Court, we will be seeing all four of them. In one form or another, they can be found in many legal systems. Whenever the issue involves human rights, many people will be drawn to Heroes. Whenever the issue involves national security, many people will embrace the Soldier. If society is in the midst of flux, or if the judges are not sure what they are doing, the Minimalist will have a great deal of appeal. And when social controversy is at its height, some people might insist, with the Mute, that silence is golden.

We have seen that as a matter of principle, it makes no sense to adopt a particular Persona for all occasions, and indeed few people do so. The right Persona is a product of the right theory of interpretation. If broad judicial deference to the political process emerges from the right theory, then it is best to be a Soldier. But on at least some occasions, the violation of the Constitution will be clear, and a Soldier must become a Hero. If we agree that the meaning of the Constitution is fixed by the original understanding, then judges must be Heroes on some occasions and Soldiers on others. If we agree that the meaning of the Constitution legitimately evolves, and that it is appropriate for judges to protect those who are subject to pervasive hostility and prejudice, then we will embrace the Hero in some cases and the Soldier in others. I have argued on behalf of a general enthusiasm for the Minimalist, on the ground that minimalism is well suited to the institutional virtues and limits of the judiciary. But minimalism is not a complete theory of interpretation, and it is hardly an approach for all times and all seasons.

Theories of interpretation are one thing; rules of attraction are another. In life and in law, people have immediate enthusiasm for certain types—for the bold (and impressive and eye-catching), for the deferential (and calm and polite), for the cautious (and incremental and humble), for the silent (and mysterious and possibly elegant). The enthusiasm may or may not fit with people's considered view about the appropriate type. In romance, you might be drawn to people who are charismatic; you might like rogues. But maybe they are not best for you, and maybe you are well aware of that fact. In constitutional law, you might be initially inclined to favor the Hero, and a loud voice in your head might claim that they are hard to resist. But on reflection, you might think that the Soldier or the Minimalist is usually best. I cannot prove the point here, but I believe that initial enthusiasms, drawing people to one or another Persona, play a large role in constitutional law, and those enthusiasms are not easy to dislodge with argument.

My topic here has been constitutional law and the federal judiciary, but it should be plain that the Personae can be located in many domains of social life. In politics, we can certainly find analogues to Heroes, Minimalists, and Mutes. In fact, Heroes and Minimalists, in particular, define much of modern political life. At least in political campaigns, many people are drawn to the Hero, who is the most compelling of political figures; but the Minimalist also has unmistakable appeal.

If we understand Heroes as those with large-scale visions, and a willingness and an ability to implement them, we can see Abraham Lincoln, Franklin Delano Roosevelt, and Ronald Reagan as defining presidential Heroes. All three were transformational presidents. At key points in their various campaigns, and certainly at important stages of their presidencies, bold strokes and large-scale thinking defined their public lives.

With his Emancipation Proclamation, of course, Lincoln set out ideals of freedom and dignity that have helped to define the United States ever since. Those ideals have had ramifying effects in countless areas of American life, including equality on the basis of sex, disability, and sexual orientation. With his New Deal, and eventually his Second Bill of Rights, Roosevelt defined a novel conception of American self-government, one that has largely sustained itself over time. Consider the heroic nature of these words, which Roosevelt offered as a kind of summary of his presidency:

> This Republic had its beginning, and grew to its present strength, under the protection of certain inalienable political rights—among them the right of free speech, free press, free worship, trial by jury, freedom from unreasonable searches and seizures. They were our rights to life and liberty.
>
> As our Nation has grown in size and stature, however—as our industrial economy expanded—these political rights proved inadequate to assure us equality in the pursuit of happiness.
>
> We have come to a clear realization of the fact that true individual freedom cannot exist without economic security and independence. "Necessitous men are not free men." People who are hungry and out of a job are the stuff of which dictatorships are made.
>
> In our day these economic truths have become accepted as self-evident. We have accepted, so to speak, a second Bill of Rights under which a new basis of security and prosperity can be established for all regardless of station, race, or creed.

Among these are:

The right to a useful and remunerative job in the industries or shops or farms or mines of the Nation;

The right to earn enough to provide adequate food and clothing and recreation;

The right of every farmer to raise and sell his products at a return which will give him and his family a decent living;

The right of every businessman, large and small, to trade in an atmosphere of freedom from unfair competition and domination by monopolies at home or abroad;

The right of every family to a decent home;

The right to adequate medical care and the opportunity to achieve and enjoy good health;

The right to adequate protection from the economic fears of old age, sickness, accident, and unemployment;

The right to a good education.

All of these rights spell security. And after this war is won we must be prepared to move forward, in the implementation of these rights, to new goals of human happiness and well-being.[1]

For present purposes, what makes these words noteworthy is their sheer boldness and size. With his efforts to reduce the authority of the federal government, and to win the Cold War, Reagan also cut a singularly heroic figure. In substance, of course, his views were a sharp contrast with Roosevelt, but in terms of Persona, they were not so far apart (as Reagan was well aware). Reagan argued for a party that would raise "a banner of no pale pastels, but bold colors." Consider his heroic words at the inception of his political career, in 1964:

This is the issue of this election: Whether we believe in our capacity for self-government or whether we abandon the American revolution and confess that a little intellectual elite in a far-distant capitol can plan our lives for us better than we can plan them ourselves.

You and I are told increasingly we have to choose between a left or right. Well I'd like to suggest there is no such thing as a left or right. There's only an up or down—[up] man's old—old-aged dream, the ultimate in individual freedom consistent with law and order, or down to the ant heap of totalitarianism. And regardless of their sincerity, their humanitarian motives, those who would trade our freedom for security have embarked on this downward course.[2]

Many of those who were drawn to Reagan, and who continue to admire him, cherish his heroic Persona. In any election, some voters seek large figures, who call for big, bold strokes and who will break from the status quo, perhaps to return to a better era, perhaps to create one that has no precedents—in either, some kind of shining city on a hill.

In politics, Minimalists are less likely to attract voters than Heroes; few people are likely to want to devote their time and effort to the election of a Minimalist. But if we think that the nation is on the right course, or if we are suspicious of transformation, we might well prefer Minimalists to Heroes, even in the Oval Office. Burkeanism has an important place in the public domain. And if we define Minimalists as those who seek incremental movements, and who prize stability, we can see Gerald Ford, George H. W. Bush, and Bill Clinton as presidential exemplars. Those who are suspicious of large changes in course, and who think that continuity is an important virtue, will have much to say in favor of one or more of these presidents.

To be sure, no president can be silent, but all political figures occasionally play the Mute, in the sense that they remain quiet on certain questions on the ground that any statement at all can create real trouble. Franklin Delano Roosevelt was a Hero, but he was famously reluctant to answer what he dismissed as "What if?" questions. Calvin Coolidge, known as Silent Cal, was the canonical presidential Mute, and every president is aware that silence can be golden. Journalists are immensely frustrated by political Mutes, but it is often the right practice. Often what you don't say can't hurt you—or the nation as a whole. There is honor in silence.

The analogy to Soldiers is the most complex and in many ways the most challenging. In democracies, some political figures purport to channel the will of the people, and essentially to take instructions. They are Soldiers in the sense that they are following the orders of their superiors: We the People. Many political scientists and economists insist that politicians generally seek to maximize their chances of reelection. If so, then we might be able to see many political figures as essentially Soldiers. And of course there is a familiar conception of political representation, which regards elected officials as charged with implementing the (informed) views of the public. Certainly it is true that public officials are keenly alert to political constraints on what they can do. Those constraints tend to turn them into Soldiers.

With respect to judges, political figures, corporate executives, and others, it would be interesting to test the psychological claim that I have ventured here, which is that for many people, one or another Persona has a kind of magnetic attraction—so much so that the justification offered on its behalf is an after-the-fact rationalization, the tail that wags the dog. True, the attraction might turn out to be justified—but perhaps not. Bold figures often have a lot of appeal. They might even be irresistible. But they can create real trouble; sometimes a nation does best to avoid Heroes. Nor are humility and caution virtues for all seasons. (Roosevelt said in 1932: "The country needs and, unless I mistake its temper, the country demands bold, persistent experimentation. It is common sense to take a method and try it: If it fails, admit it frankly and try another. But above all, try something.") And Soldiers sometimes execute horrific orders.

The case for one or another Persona depends on the arguments made on its behalf, not on psychological inclinations. Different circumstances require different Personae. To know which is best, we need to investigate the circumstances. But in politics and law, as in ordinary life, the rules of attraction, rather than the arguments, often end up running the show.

Acknowledgments

. . .

I have been working on the ideas in this book for many years, and I owe thanks to countless friends and colleagues for indispensable discussions. Thanks go first and foremost to Geoffrey Stone, editor of the series in which this book appears; I am grateful to Geof for his extraordinary guidance and insight, and even more for his friendship. For helpful discussions and comments on the argument of one or more of the chapters, I single out Christine Jolls, Frank Michelman, Martha Nussbaum, Eric Posner, Richard Posner, Mark Tushnet, the late Edna Ullmann-Margalit, and Adrian Vermeule. Thanks also to several anonymous reviewers for valuable comments and suggestions. My editor, David McBride, offered terrific suggestions that greatly improved the manuscript. Thanks too to my agent, Sarah Chalfant, for help and guidance of many kinds. Mary Schnoor provided valuable research assistance.

Though this book celebrates minimalism, I know that some people will not join in the celebration. In 2008, when I was first dating my now-wife, Samantha Power, I explained to her what minimalism was all about. Her response was simple: "Minimalism sucks." She's a Hero, and a hero, and I dedicate the book to her, with love and admiration.

An early version of chapter 1 appeared as *Constitutional Personae*, 2013 SUPREME COURT REVIEW 1. For chapter 2, I have drawn on parts of the first chapter of A CONSTITUTION OF MANY MINDS (2009) and on an essay appearing in Constitutional Commentary (2015). An early version of chapter 3 appeared as *Burkean Minimalism*, 105 MICH L. REV. 353 (2006). Chapter 4 draws on the more extensive treatment in *Unanimity and Dissent on the Supreme Court*, 100 CORNELL L. REV. 765 (2015). In all cases, the preliminary discussions have been thoroughly revised and rethought.

Notes

. . .

CHAPTER ONE: CONSTITUTIONAL PERSONAE

1. *See* RONALD DWORKIN, LAW'S EMPIRE 238–75 (1985).
2. JOHN HART ELY, DEMOCRACY AND DISTRUST, at v (1980).
3. Lochner v. New York, 198 U.S. 45, 76 (1905) (Holmes, J., dissenting).
4. Abrams v. United States, 250 U.S. 616, 630 (1911) (Holmes, J., dissenting).
5. *See* ADRIAN VERMEULE, JUDGING UNDER UNCERTAINTY (2006).
6. District of Columbia v. Heller, 554 U.S. 570 (2008).
7. Edmund Burke, *Reflections on the Revolution in France*, in THE PORTABLE EDMUND BURKE 416, 456–57 (Isaac Kramnick ed., 1999).
8. *See* ALEXANDER BICKEL, THE LEAST DANGEROUS BRANCH (1965).
9. *See* Gerald Gunther, *The Subtle Vices of the "Passive Virtues,"* 64 COLUM. L. REV. 1, 3 (1964).

CHAPTER TWO: INTERPRETATION

1. Larry Alexander, *Simple-Minded Originalism* (2008), available at http://papers.ssrn.com/so13/papers.cfm?abstract_id=1235722.

2. *See* Walter Benn Michaels, *A Defense of Old Originalism*, 31 WESTERN
   NEW ENGLAND LAW REVIEW 21, 21 (2009). For an analogous
   argument, see STEVEN SMITH, LAW'S QUANDARY (2007); for an
   analogous argument with a focus on meaning rather than intentions, see
   Gary Lawson, *On Reading Recipes . . . and Constitutions*, 85 GEO. L.J.
   1823 (1997). For an instructive discussion, also with an emphasis on
   meaning, see Lawrence Solum, *Semantic Originalism* (2008), available at
   http://papers.ssrn.com/so13/papers.cfm?abstract_id=1120244.
3. *See* District of Columbia v. Heller, 554 US 570 (2008). Grice similarly
   distinguishes between "speaker's meaning" and "sentence meaning." See
   H. P. Grice, *Utterer's Meaning, Sentence-Meaning, and Word Meaning*, 4
   FOUND. LANGUAGE 225, 225 (1968).
4. *Id.*
5. Oliver Wendell Holmes, *The Theory of Legal Interpretation*, 12 HARV
   L. REV. 417 (1899). See Lawrence Solum, *Semantic Originalism* 5 (2008),
   available at http://papers.ssrn.com/so13/papers.cfm?abstract_
   id=1120244: "The argument for clause meaning will be elaborated at
   length, but the intuitive idea is simple. The constitution was drafted and
   ratified by a multitude: many different individuals at different times and
   places. The intentional mental states of the multitude with respect to a
   given constitutional provision (their purposes, hopes, fears, expectations,
   and so forth) will themselves be multitudinous and inaccessible.
   Multitudinous, because different framers and ratifiers had different
   intentions, with the consequence that intentions alone cannot fix
   consistent (noncontradictory and not radically ambiguous) semantic
   content. Inaccessible, because those who were expected to engage in
   constitutional practice (the judges, officials, and citizens of the United
   States of American for an indefinite future) would have found the
   multitudinous intentions epistemically inaccessible." Solum adds: "The
   possibility of constitutional communication was created by the fact that
   the framers and ratifiers could rely on the accessibility of the public
   meaning (or conventional semantic meaning) of the words, phrases, and
   clauses that constitute the Constitution. Not only can such public
   meanings enable constitutional communication at the time a given
   constitutional provisions is drafted, approved, and first implemented, such
   meanings can also become stable over time or be recovered if they are lost.
   In other words, under normal conditions successful constitutional

communication requires reliance by the drafters, ratifiers, and interpreters on the original public meaning of the words and phrases." *Id.*

6. Available at http://legalaffairs.org/webexclusive/debateclub_cie0505 .msp.

7. I am bracketing the question whether that is the right way to understand them. The only suggestion is that there is a strong argument against originalism if, understood in a certain way, it makes our constitutional system worse. It remains possible that some understandings of originalism would not have that effect. See JACK BALKIN, LIVING ORIGINALISM (2011).

8. *See* JACK BALKIN, LIVING ORIGINALISM (2012).

9. *See* H. Jefferson Powell, *The Original Understanding of Original Intent*, 98 HARVARD L. REV. 885 (1985).

10. *See* RONALD DWORKIN, LAW'S EMPIRE (1985).

11. RONALD DWORKIN, LAW'S EMPIRE (1985).

12. *See* KEITH WHITTINGTON, CONSTITUTIONAL CONSTRUCTION (1999); JACK BALKIN, LIVING ORIGINALISM (2012).

13. *See* Lawrence Solum, *The Interpretation-Construction Distinction*, 27 CONSTITUTIONAL COMMENTARY 95 (2010). As Solum emphasizes, the distinction has a long history and has been understood in several different ways.

14. *Id.* at 104.

CHAPTER THREE: BURKEAN MINIMALISM

1. Youngstown Sheet & Tube Co. v. Sawyer, 343 U.S. 579 (1952) (Frankfurter, J., concurring).

2. Edmund Burke, *Reflections on the Revolution in France*, in THE PORTABLE EDMUND BURKE 416–51 (Isaac Kramnick ed. 1999).

3. *See* the discussion of "norms of partiality" in EDNA ULLMANN-MARGALIT, THE EMERGENCE OF NORMS (1977).

4 For a superb discussion, see Edna Ullmann-Margalit, *The Invisible Hand and the Cunning of Reason*, 64 SOCIAL RESEARCH 181 (1997).

5. *See* DAVID A. STRAUSS, THE COMMON LAW CONSTITUTION (2011).

6. *See* Michael H. v. Gerald D., 491 U.S. 110 (1989).
7. Youngstown Sheet & Tube Co. v. Sawyer, 343 U.S. 579 (1952) (Frankfurter, J., concurring).
8. Leon Kass, *The Wisdom of Repugnance*, in THE ETHICS OF HUMAN CLONING 19 (Leon Kass and James W. Wilson eds. 1998).
9. *See* Oliver Wendell Holmes, *The Path of the Law*, 10 HARV. L. REV. 457 (1897).
10. THE FEDERALIST, NO. 14.
11. Letter from Thomas Jefferson to Samuel Kercheval (July 12, 1816), reprinted in THE PORTABLE THOMAS JEFFERSON 552, 559 (M. Peterson ed. 1977). Note, however, that Jefferson is speaking of experience, not of a priori reasoning (or "book-reading").
12. Blaise Pascal, *Preface to the Treatise on Vacuum*, in THOUGHTS, LETTERS, AND MINOR WORKS 444, 449 (Charles W. Eliot ed., M. L. Booth et al. trans., 1910).
13. JEREMY BENTHAM, HANDBOOK OF POLITICAL FALLACIES 44–45 (Harold A. Larrabee ed., 1952).
14. Youngstown Sheet & Tube Co. v. Sawyer, 343 U.S. 579, 594–55 (1952) (Frankfurter, J., concurring).

CHAPTER FOUR: UNANIMITY AND DISAGREEMENT

1. http://www.theatlantic.com/magazine/archive/2007/01/robertss-rules/305559/.
2. The original treatment is C. HERMAN PRITCHETT, THE ROOSEVELT COURT: A STUDY IN JUDICIAL POLITICS AND VALUES, 1937–1947 (1948); Pritchett noticed that "the 1941–42 term was definitely a turning point for the Roosevelt Court." *Id.* at 40. In my view, the best discussion remains Thomas Walker et al., *On the Mysterious Demise of Consensual Norm in the United States Supreme Court*, 50 J POLITICS 361 (1988). I owe a particular debt to that discussion here. An exceedingly valuable, recent treatment is PAMELA C. CORLEY ET AL., THE PUZZLE OF UNANIMITY (2013); a relevant part of that discussion can be found in Pamela C. Corley et al., *Revisiting the Roosevelt Court: The Critical Juncture from Consensus to Dissensus*, 38 J. OF SUPREME COURT HIST. 20 (2013).

3. All numbers from 1801–2009 are from LEE EPSTEIN, JEFFREY
   A. SEGAL, HAROLD J. SPAETH, & THOMAS G. WALKER, THE
   SUPREME COURT COMPENDIUM: DATA, DECISIONS, AND
   DEVELOPMENTS, 5th ed. (2012). Numbers from 2010–12 are from
   Harold J. Spaeth, Sara Benesh, Lee Epstein, Andrew D. Martin, Jeffrey
   A. Segal, & Theodore J. Ruger. 2013. Supreme Court Database, Version
   2013 Release 01. URL: http://supremecourtdatabase.org. Last accessed
   on July 12, 2014. Numbers from the 2013 term were collected by the
   author. As used here, the rate of dissent is the percentage of total
   opinions in a term that contain one or more dissenting opinions; the rate
   of concurrence is the percentage of total opinions in a term that contain
   one or more concurring opinions; and the rate of cases decided by a
   one-vote margin is the percentage of the total cases decided by a 5–4 or
   4–3 split. The total opinions in a term are taken to be all full written
   opinions, in addition to *per curiam* opinions following oral argument.
4. G. Edward White, *The Internal Powers of the Chief Justice: The
   Nineteenth-Century Legacy*, 154 U. PA. L. REV. 1463, 1466 (2006).
5. John Marshall, A Friend of the Union, quoted in JEAN EDWARD
   SMITH, JOHN MARSHALL: DEFINER OF A NATION 282 (1998). On
   the relationship between Marshall's work on behalf of unanimity and
   the Court's limited prestige, see *id.* at 282–87.
6. Bank of the United States v. Dandridge, 25 U.S. (12 Wheat.) 64, 90 (1827)
   (Marshall, C.J., dissenting), quoted in White, supra note, at 1471 n.17.
7. The Nereide, 13 U.S. (9 Cranch) 388, 455 (1815) (Story, J., dissenting),
   quoted in *id.*
8. Mason v. Haile, 25 U.S. (12 Wheat.) 370, 379 (1827) (Washington, J.,
   dissenting), quoted in *id.*
9. *Letter from Thomas Jefferson to William Johnson* (Oct. 27, 1822), in THE
   WRITINGS OF THOMAS JEFFERSON, 1816–1826, at 225, quoted in
   White, supra note, at 1473.
10. *Letter from William Johnson to Thomas Jefferson* (Dec. 10, 1822), quoted
    in DONALD G. MORGAN, JUSTICE WILLIAM JOHNSON: THE FIRST
    DISSENTER: THE CAREER AND CONSTITUTIONAL PHILOSOPHY OF A
    JEFFERSONIAN JUDGE 181–82 (1954), quoted in White, supra note, at 1473.
11. O'Brien, supra note, at 93.
12. Quoted in O'Brien, supra note, at 93.

13. Quoted in Corley et al., supra note, at 31.
14. Quoted in HENRY J. ABRAHAM, THE JUDICIAL PROCESS 224, 5th ed. (1986), Walker et al., supra note, at 381.
15. *Id.*
16. Quoted in Walker et al., supra note, at 379.
17. Pamela C. Corley, Amy Steigerwalt, & Artemus Ward, *Revisiting the Roosevelt Court: The Critical Juncture from Consensus to Dissensus*, 38 J. SUP. CT. HIST. 22 (2013).
18. Quoted in Corley et al., supra note, at 40.
19. Quoted in O'Brien, supra note, at 1078.
20. Walker et al., supra note, at 378.
21. Brennan, supra note, at 438.
22. L. HAND, THE BILL OF RIGHTS 72 (1958).
23. 545 U.S. 469 (2005).
24. Michael F. Salamone, *Judicial Consensus and Public Opinion: Conditional Response to Supreme Court Majority Size*, 20 POL. RES. Q. 1 (2013).
25. THOMAS G. HANSFORD & JAMES F. SPRIGGS, THE POLITICS OF PRECEDENT ON THE U.S. SUPREME COURT 90–92 (2006).
26. James F. Spriggs, II & Thomas G. Hansford, *Explaining the Overruling of U.S. Supreme Court Precedent*, 63 J. POLITICS 1091, 1104–5 (2001).
27. Quoted in *Chief Justice Says His Goal Is More Consensus on the Court*, N.Y. TIMES, May 22, 2006, at A16. From John Roberts's commencement address at Georgetown University Law Center.

CLOSING WORDS

1. The speech is quoted and discussed in detail in CASS R. SUNSTEIN, THE SECOND BILL OF RIGHTS (2006).
2. The speech can be found in many places; it is available, for example, at http://www.reagan.utexas.edu/archives/reference/timechoosing.html.

Index

. . .

Figures and tables are indicated by "f" and "t" following page numbers.

conservative Heroes, 8, 32, 72, 74
constitutional interpretation
and, 50, 52
defined, 2, 5
equality issues and, 71
liberal Heroes, 73
libertarian views and, 9–10
in *Lochner* era, 113
Minimalists' view of, 25
moral reading of
Constitution by, 55
Mutes' view of, 26
originalists and
nonoriginalists as, 6
original meaning and, 6, 10, 51, 146
in political life, 146–150
as preferred Persona, 9, 146
promoting equality, 5–6
realignment to status quo before
New Deal and, 6
recess appointments and, 30
relationship with Burkean
Minimalists, 85, 86, 88,
96, 99–102
relationship with Minimalists, 10
relationship with Mutes, 20, 27
relationship with Rational
Minimalists, 90
relationship with Soldiers, 7, 14,
59–60, 62, 110, 115, 142, 145
in same-sex marriage case, 28, 36,
78, 86, 91, 101
in specific areas of law, 8, 37, 145
theoretical ambition of, 6
traditions and, 69, 85
High salience, Court decisions
with, 135

Hollingsworth v. Perry, 23, 28, 34
Holmes, Oliver Wendell
as great dissenter, 113, 119
as Hero, 12
in *Lochner* dissent, 85, 87, 103–104
morality and, 32, 100
rejecting subjective intent, 49
as Soldier, 11, 14, 39, 103–104, 113, 129
theories of construction and, 59
Hours of work, 7, 39, 113
Hubris, xiv, 14, 24, 25, 26, 39, 91
Hughes, Charles Evans, 118, 119, 122
Human rights, 64, 145
Humility, xiv, 2, 16, 17, 21, 25, 26, 40,
78, 146, 150
Hypocrisy, 39

Ideology and choice of
Personae, 38–40
Incorporation doctrine, 85
Incrementalism, 17, 70, 74–76. *See
also* Case-by-case adjudication
Independent regulatory
agencies, 68, 98
Interpretation. *See* Constitutional
interpretation

Jackson, Robert, 121, 123
Japanese internment during World
War II, 31
Jay, John, 116
Jefferson, Thomas, 104, 117–118, 129
Johnson, William, 117–118
Judicial deference, 12–13, 32, 33, 39,
59, 145
Judicial discretion, 17, 50, 54, 56, 62
Judicial restraint, 11, 80–81